Change Buyer Behavior And Sell More Annuities

Rational

Emotional

Illusions

Jack Marrion

This book is for educational purposes only and does not provide legal, tax, or investment advice. Readers should consult own advisor for their personal situation. Any laws or regulations cited have been edited and summarized for clarity's sake. Any names used in this publication are fictional and have no relationship to any person living or dead. Information is from sources believed accurate but is not warranted.

Printed in the United States of America

First Printing, January 2009

ISBN   0-9728251-2-6

Advantage Compendium   (314) 434-6030
2187 Butterfield Court
St. Louis MO 63043   jack.marrion@gmail.com

Change Buyer Behavior And Sell More Annuities

The Author

Jack Marrion's research and insights have been featured in hundreds of publications including *Business Week, Kiplinger, Smart Money* and *The Wall Street Journal*; he is a frequent speaker and media guest, as well as an industry columnist. He has an M.B.A. from the University of Missouri and his doctoral studies in the area of cognitive bias in consumer decision-making form the basis for this his fifth book.

Prior to forming the Advantage Compendium Mr. Marrion was president of an investment broker/dealer with offices in nine states, and formerly vice president of a life insurance company and vice president of an NYSE investment banking firm.

Chapter 1 – Introduction

This book was written to help you close more annuity sales. It explains why consumers sometimes do not buy annuities and what you can do to help close the sale. It is designed to be practical instead of theoretical, so that when you are sitting down with a consumer, and run into trouble, hopefully something from the book will come to mind and help you close the sale.

The book is based on years of both practical and academic research. On the academic side I have taken the results of hundreds of studies showing how consumers actually make decisions. Many of these results have been implemented in other industries and have resulted in increased sales, but they have not been used in the annuity or financial world. All I have done is taken what is working elsewhere and applied it to the annuity sale. But this book is not a schoolbook. It is supposed to help you sell more in the real world by covering what is missing in almost all annuity training and sales literature.

How Consumers Really Make Decisions

If I were to ask you why consumers buy fixed annuities you might say it is because of the safety from market risk or maybe because of the guarantees or perhaps due to the tax-deferral element. Indeed, there are a number of rational reasons to purchase a fixed annuity, and these are almost never the real reason behind the purchase.

Some Rational Reasons To Buy Fixed Annuities
- Higher Potential Yields
- No Market-Risk of Loss
- Tax-Deferred Interest
- Lifetime Income Options
- Minimum Guaranteed Return
- Avoid Probate

Wall Street and its economists all seem to treat consumers as if they are computers. They assume that all of us make rational financial decisions to maximize the economic utility of any situation. They give us oceans of charts, tidal waves of slides and fathoms of math columns all designed to prove they have the most rational answer. But consumers do not make rational decisions. They make normal decisions. Consumer decisions contain some rational pieces, but they also are influenced by the emotions at the time of the decision and memories of the past that are considered as facts but may be illusions. These rational pieces, behavioral elements and illusions combine in the decision-making process and the interaction of these three areas results in a decision.

3 Elements Of A Decision

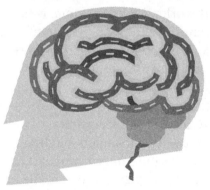

Rational

Emotional

Illusions

The standard annuity training courses and books concentrate almost solely on the rational reasons why people buy annuities and ignore the other parts. The result is we often talk on a purely rational level, while the prospect is moving between different levels, and the result is a misconnection – and often no sale. This book will help you connect with prospects on all levels and the better you can connect with the consumer the more likely you are to close the sale.

What This Book Is

The book is broadly divided into three parts. The first part lists the rational reasons for buying fixed annuities and how bounded rationality can keep even the most rational consumer from making the best decision for their situation. I will talk about how to expand a prospect's mind to help realize why a fixed annuity makes sense.

The second part deals with beliefs that consumers think are factual when they are often illusions. The book will give you arguments and ammunition to tear down the illusionary walls that sometimes get in the way of the sale.

The third part tells you how to react when the consumer is emotionally objecting to the annuity purchase. It gives you an understanding of what is going on in the consumer's mind, why the consumer may be thinking that way, and steps you can take to change the consumer's mind.

This is not a textbook and you do not need a degree in psychology to understand it, just as you do not need a degree in engineering to drive a car. A lot of this book is simply taking results from other places and translating them into the annuity world. If someone wants to dig deeper I have included any academic sources for many of the topics discussed.

What This Book Is Not

This is not An Introduction to Annuities. When I mention minimum guarantees or surrender charges or tax-deferral or participation rates I am assuming the reader has at least a basic understanding of what it all means. Although the general ideas mentioned in this book may be used to sell anything the focus is on selling fixed annuities.

This book is not Sales Training 101. The goal of the book is to help you close more annuity sales when you are sitting across from the consumer. I say nothing about how to prospect, I do not create presentation scripts, and I do not have sections on "overcoming objections" or "closing techniques." What I have found is when you connect with the consumer – if you do it right – you do not get objections that are really excuses and there is no "close" because the entire process is the consumer doing their own close.

I would love to be able to say "here is the sales script to guarantee a sale" or "when the consumer raises concern #24 you should respond with answer #31" but every sales situation is a little different and every consumer has a unique background that influences their decisions, so you need to be able to adapt. However, there are common rational boundaries, shared illusions, and typical human behaviors that are almost universal. If you understand the basics that are covered in this book it will make it easier to connect with the consumer and adapt.

This is not to say that this book will allow you to close every consumer you meet. There are situations where an annuity is not the correct solution for the consumer's needs and this book will not help you sell someone that has no need for an annuity. What this book will do is allow you to quickly tell when the consumer is not an annuity buyer so you may move on to a better prospect.

Whether There Is A Sale Comes Down To This
Whether a consumer is buying an ice cream cone or an annuity, or not buying an ice cream cone or an annuity, the ultimate reason for all decisions is either to feel good or avoid feeling bad. This book will help you make consumers avoid feeling bad by buying an annuity.

Who Are "You"?
This book is written for folks that sell annuities to consumers. You are called annuity producers, agents, financial service professionals, and several other names. I call you "representatives" because in this changing financial picture you are truly becoming the consumer's representative in understanding the annuity world.

How Do You Read This Book?

The end of this chapter lists objections that have killed annuity sales for many representatives. The page containing a solution to the problem follows the questions. You could simply turn to these pages when you get into trouble, find the right "treatment" and generally use the book as a reference. I think you will get more out of it if you read the book from start to finish because the whole book should give you a better understanding of what is actually going on in the head of the consumer across the table from you.

Four Main Decision Points To Appreciate

Consumers Buy From People They Like

We tend to like people that are similar to us and have an attractive personality. In a sales world it translates into consumers working with representatives that are likeable. Indeed, although we respect knowledge, a typical consumer would rather work with a likeable barely competent representative than a brilliant jerk. It may also mean being likeable could trump a competitor's advantages if the competitor is perceived as less likable.

Increasing likeability can increase sales

What are the implications for representatives? How you relate to others is more important than product knowledge, and if you are competing against a better rate you may still triumph by being more likeable. Consumers want to buy from people they are comfortable with and knowing you are reachable and going to be there for them if they need you may well be worth more than a competitor's extra half percentage of yield.

None of this means that one can succeed on "likes alone." The representative still needs to meet the requirements of their job; incompetence will eventually run you out of business regardless of how nice you are. However, increasing likeability can mean both increasing sales and decreasing costs, and everyone likes that.

Emotional Decision Is Often Made Before Rational One

When we are presented with an unfamiliar situation we hear murmurs in our minds of the goodness or badness of the new situation. Before we have time to think about the merits of the decision our feelings are quickly assessing it on an emotional level and causing us to react. The reason why is we subconsciously create mental rules of thumb using decisions that worked well in the past to deal with the new and unfamiliar.

This was a good thing in prehistoric times. Pausing to assess the logical reasons why the saber tooth tiger may or may not attack – instead of giving into the impulse to run away – often would have meant we were lunch for the tiger. Unfortunately our brains still trigger the same type of reactions today. An attack on our financial safety is emotionally viewed as an attack by a saber tooth tiger, with the result that we often react to the imagined size of the threat instead of determining the best response.

The representative needs to direct the consumer's emotional reaction so that it does not get in the way of making the sale. One way is to frame the situation in a way that the old rule of thumb does not apply. It would be saying, "I know you lost money the last time the stock market went down but this time you are in a fixed annuity and you are not at market risk." The quickest way to stop a bad rule of thumb from being used is to show that it does not apply to the new situation.

We Need Reference Points (Zero May Not Be Your Hero)

The great thing about an index annuity is the worse that can happen is you may get zero interest next year, but at least you cannot lose interest. This has been a key point of index annuities since day one, but it may stop the purchase if mishandled.

A study found that people found a bet where they could win $9 or lose 5¢ to be much more attractive than one where they could win $9 or lose nothing. Why would the possibility of losing money be more attractive than a zero loss?

We tend to judge things by the direction and magnitude of their movement from a reference point. Positive numbers show movement forward, negative numbers show movement backwards. If one number is larger than the other we feel the number with the greater magnitude is showing the direction. Nine dollars is larger than 5¢, so the direction with $9 is subconsciously perceived as the winning direction. Zero does not have a direction so there is nothing to compare magnitudes with; the $9 just sits there and cannot be evaluated.

Rather than describing a potential index annuity return by saying "you could earn from zero to 7% next year (referring to the interest cap)" it might be better to say "you could earn up to 5% more than your bank CD or at worse 2% less" if the bank CD is paying 2%."

In a way paying a living benefit rider charge could help close annuity sales because you can offer distinct reference points – "you could earn up to 7% if the index goes up or lose up to 0.45% (the rider charge) if the index goes down." Since a possible 7% gain is a much larger positive number than the 0.45% negative loss it justifies why a positive decision should be made.

Smart People Are Not Fully Rational Either
The doctor, engineer or teacher across the table may have a higher IQ than the average consumer, but they still succumb to biases, although sometimes to a lesser degree. Their education may make them more comfortable with the realities of probabilities, and they may be able to spot a gap in logic quicker, but they still are affected by emotions and illusions.

Sales Points

- Decisions consist of rational points, emotional behavior and illusion. If you only connect with one or two elements you may not close the sale

- Increasing likeability can increase sales

- How you relate to others is more important than product knowledge

Background Sources

Consumers Buy From People They Like
Casciaro, T. & Sousa Lobo. 2005. Competent Jerks, Lovable Fools, and the Formation of Social Networks. *Harvard Business Review*. 6:92

Youngme Moon. 2005. Break Free From The Product Life Cycle, *Harvard Business Review*. 5:87

Zero May Not Be Your Hero
Slovic, P., Finucane, Peters & MacGregor. 2002. The affect heuristic. *Heuristics and Biases: The Psychology of Intuitive Judgment*. New York. Cambridge University Press. 397-420

Stewart, Neil *etal*. 2003. Prospect Relativity: How choice options influence decision under risk. *Journal of Experimental Psychology*. 132.1:23–46

Smart People Are Not Fully Rational Either
Stanovich, Keith, Richard F. West. 2008. On the relative independence of thinking biases and cognitive ability. *Journal of Personality and Social Psychology*. 94.4:672–695

Here are 21 situations that have killed annuity sales (and the page with the solution)

How annuity returns compare with CDs (15)

Most consumers could care less about tax-deferral; here is how to make them care (22)

The three main fixed annuity risks are... (43)

What determines renewal rates (49)

What to say to a consumer that says bank rates are going up (73)

How to make a competitor's higher yield seem smaller (74)

What can be done with a know-it-all prospect (116)

Why annuities sales are easier when the stock market is up (118)

How to make gains seem bigger and losses smaller (125)

Why using the phrase "trading in last-year's model" encourages annuity exchanges (128)

How to take away the consumer's CD bliss (131)

How a Gambling Feeling can result in a long-term-care or life insurance sale (131)

Does the consumer believe in hot streaks or that a change is due? Their answer tells you which is the best sales approach (132)

Why "no stock market risk" is the wrong way to introduce fixed annuities (143)

Chapter 2 – Rational Boundaries

A little over 60 years ago a wise man named Herbert Simon figured out people could never make perfect decisions because we do not have perfect information about all the possible alternatives. As people we cannot possibly know everything there is to know because what we know is limited by our experiences and learning, and even if we could be a walking encyclopedia we cannot know everything we do not know because the future is unwritten. So even when we try to make the most rational decisions possible we have *bounded rationality* meaning there are limits to what we know so that even our rational decisions are bounded or limited and cannot be perfect. Deep, isn't it?

The concept of bounded rationality affects annuity buyers in two ways. The first and foremost significant effect is consumers are often not even aware of what annuities can do for them so they are not even a part of the financial decision process. To show my point, if you are trying to put out a fire on a beach and the only thing you have been taught is that sand puts out fires you probably would be throwing buckets of sand on the fire instead of using water. However, once you were aware of how well water worked you might start using water as an extinguisher. The bounds of your rational mind were expanded and now you would consider water if the situation rose again.

I have found the typical consumer is more aware of certificates of deposits, stock, bonds and mutual funds than they are of annuities. I have found the typical financial advisor and financial reporter are also more aware of certificates of deposits, stock, bonds and mutual funds than they are of annuities. All three are limited by bounded rationality, but the consumer is typically not choosing the annuity because they are not aware of them. The financial advisor and financial reporter often do not choose the annuity because they have already made their decision not to use or like annuities and are not open to challenges.

It is enabling the consumer to think "I was right to not buy a variable annuity in the past, but now they offer guaranteed lifetime benefits so I can buy one today" or "I was right not to buy a fixed annuity before, but now that I am retired the guarantees make sense."

You were right then and you are right now!

The new information the representative is providing enables the consumer that purchased the CD or mutual fund or oil well a few years ago to conclude that buying an annuity today does not mean admitting they were wrong not to buy one in the past because today is different.

Expanded Boundaries

Consumers often do not buy annuities because they are unaware of them, and by expanding the consumer's knowledge an annuity purchase often results. Consumers also may not buy annuities today because they decided not to buy one yesterday, and to buy one today would force them to admit they were wrong. The representative needs to first determine which type of consumer they are dealing with by asking, "Are you familiar with annuities?" If the answer is no, the representative educates the consumer. If the answer is yes, and the consumer says they do not like annuities, the representative must find out what it is the consumer does not like and then show the consumer why circumstances have changed so that the consumer can be right about liking the representative's annuity.

The Rational Reasons

I said at the start of the book that rational reasons are almost never the real or only reason behind the annuity purchase, but the representative still needs to provide rational reasons to buy the annuity. This is because the consumer needs to walk away with rational justifications for the purchase.

You may say you bought the Lexus because it has side airbags, ABS brakes and a high customer satisfaction rating, but so does my Hyundai. The real reason you bought the Lexus might be because it makes you feel successful, but folks usually need rational reasons to justify a decision based on feelings.

The decision to buy an annuity, like most other decisions, is based on either trying to feel good or to avoid feeling bad, but your rational side needs rational reasons to justify the purchase, especially if the purchase involves a change of mind. This chapter is designed to provide those rational reasons in different forms so the buyer can say "here is why I bought the annuity."

Rational Reasons To Buy Fixed Annuities

To Earn Potentially Higher Yields
Whether the yield is provided by a stated rate or stated participation in an index, the hope is that the annuity will provide a higher interest yield than where the money might otherwise go.

5 Year Annualized Average Returns *

	Fixed Rate Annuity	Taxable Bond Fds	Indexed Annuity	1 Yr CD
92-97	6.01	6.70		4.72
93-98	5.71	6.33		5.08
94-99	5.63	6.82		5.60
95-00	5.66	5.46		5.63
96-01	5.59	5.79		5.86
97-02	5.39	5.48	8.23	5.47
98-03	5.15	5.19	6.46	4.69
99-04	4.95	5.27	5.25	3.88
00-05	4.84	5.95	4.71	3.12
01-06	4.13	4.73	4.88	2.32
02-07	3.78	5.10	6.23	2.34

This graph compares fixed rate annuity, fixed index annuity, taxable bond fund, and certificate of deposit returns for five year periods beginning in 1992 and ending in 2007. My conclusions are that both fixed rate and fixed index annuities have been competitive with U.S. taxable bond mutual funds and CDs.

If you look at the periods from 1997 through 2007 the 5-year annualized returns for the index annuities averaged 5.79%, the average taxable bond fund return was 5.29%, the average fixed rate annualized return was 4.73%, and the CD return was 3.64%. For the periods from 1992 through 2007 the average taxable bond fund return was 5.71%, the average fixed rate annuity return was 5.18%, and the average CD return was 4.43%.

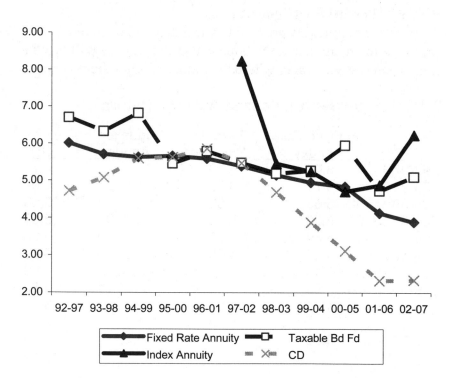

Annualized Returns for 5 Year Periods

The information is not perfect. Fixed rate annuity returns use the initial and renewal rates for 56 carriers for the first four 5-year periods; later periods reflect rates for annuities offered by "AA" or higher rated carriers not using MVA. The index annuity returns are compiled from as few as three to as many as 18 carriers, mainly because there were not a lot of index carriers in the early years. The CD data uses annualized 6-month returns until 2003 when one year CD yields were available. The footnote at the back of the chapter has all the data details.

The main point is that annuities – whether fixed rate or index – have demonstrated they provide potentially higher yields than bank CDs and can be competitive with taxable bond funds.

5 Year Annualized Average Returns *

Best's Review was the source of the earlier annuity data representing the initial and renewal rates for 56 carriers for the first four 5-year periods. Fixed rate annuity returns for later years are of Milliman, Inc. and reflect rates for annuities offered by "AA" or higher rated carriers not using MVA. The index annuity returns reflect reported annual reset returns ranging from 3 carriers for the period ending in 2002 to 18 carriers for the most recent figures. CD data is annualized 6-month yields compiled by the Federal Reserve Board. The taxable bond fund data reflects the average annualized returns for taxable bond funds for the five year periods as reported by *The Wall Street Journal*. The index annuity data reflects 1 October to 1 October periods, all other data reflects 1 July to 1 July years.

To Potentially Earn Just 2% More

In baseball we get excited about homeruns, but the winning team over the season is usually the one that puts together single base hits one at a time. In the financial world it is exciting to talk about double digit returns, but the reality is a fixed annuity – whether it is stated rate or index – will hopefully do only a percent or two better than the bank. Therefore, it is important to show consumers the power of 2% more.

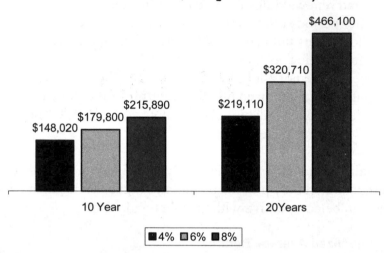

Growth of $100,000 (just 2% more)

	10 Year	20 Years
4%	$148,020	$219,110
6%	$179,800	$320,710
8%	$215,890	$466,100

■4% ▨6% ■8%

As an example, earning just 2% more each year over ten years on a $100,000 premium means at least $30,000 more in the consumer's pocket, and $30,000 more on $100,000 in ten years is real money in a believable timeframe. Earning 2% more in 20 years gives the consumer over $100,000 more in hand. And after you've identified the extra money one needs to paint a picture to show what can be with the extra money.

To Beat Certificates of Deposit Returns
A CD is a bank savings instrument with a specified maturity. Maturities can be for any term length, but most range from three months to five years. Interest may be credited daily, weekly, monthly, quarterly or yearly, and compounds and accrues until the CD is cashed or matures.

Over the last twenty years the average interest paid on certificates of deposit has ranged from around 1% to almost 18%, and these yields may swing violently between one period and the next. As an example, CD rates dropped 69% from the fall of 2000 to the fall of 2001.

CD Real Returns (After Taxes & Inflation)

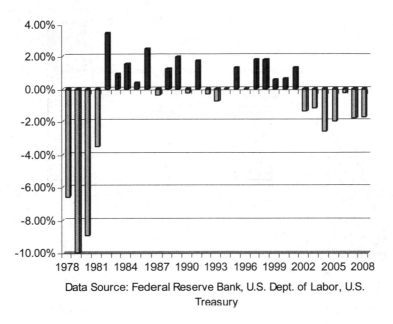

Data Source: Federal Reserve Bank, U.S. Dept. of Labor, U.S. Treasury

Certificate of deposit interest is fully taxable, even when money is compounding inside the CD. Over the past thirty years, taking into account the rate of inflation and assuming the effects of a top marginal income tax rate, real CD returns after taxes and inflation have been negative half of the time.

And If "my customer needs 10%!"

If the annuity buyer is asking for a 6%, 8%, 10% return from a fixed annuity it means the representative has screwed up. The reason it happens is because the representative has not replaced the consumer's financial reality with the representative's financial reality. We will cover this in the chapter on framing.

To Tax-Defer Interest

I was involved in a study conducted a few years ago that
discovered that 7 out of 10 consumers could care less about tax-
deferral. Think about that. Tax-deferral is a linchpin of the deferred
annuity world and yet almost three-quarters of your prospects are
tuning you out when the tax-deferral topic comes up. I think the
reason is because tax-deferral is presented like this.

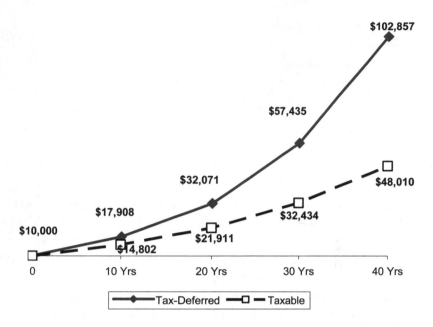

6% Growth on $10,000 - 33% Tax Rate

$102,857

$57,435

$48,010

$32,071

$32,434

$17,908

$21,911

$10,000

$14,802

| 0 | 10 Yrs | 20 Yrs | 30 Yrs | 40 Yrs |

Tax-Deferred ▬▫▬ Taxable

The first problem is this example is not specific to the consumer. Most of the tax-deferral charts all say the same thing, that tax-deferral means you will have "more money someday" and boy, is that ethereal. The other huge problem is everybody knows those deferred taxes need to be paid back someday by someone.

An 80 year old probably will not be overly impressed by showing how much more money they will have in 30 years thanks to tax-deferral, and even if a 52 year old realizes that tax-deferral could mean they have twice as much money by age 92 their overriding thought might be paying taxes on that $92,000 of deferred interest.

There are a couple of different ways to make tax-deferral meaningful for the annuity prospect sitting across the able. One way is to make tax-deferral relevant.

21

Everyone living amongst toll roads knows what a pain tollbooths are. It's not only the cost of the toll; it is the inconvenience of pulling into a line of cars, fishing for change, and interrupting your trip. Toll roads using an Easy-Pass type toll system mean you do not have to stop and fiddle for change so your trip is not interrupted. You will still be charged tolls, but you will settle up down the road and you often get a discount on the tolls that the cash people pay.

Tax-deferral is like having an IRS Easy-Pass. You do not have to fiddle with reporting interest each year and your financial trip is not interrupted by demands for cash. Sure, you will need to settle accounts when you decide to end the tax-deferral, but it will be you deciding when it is convenient to pay the taxes, and due to the extra interest earned on the money that would have gone to taxes each year you may very well wind up paying less than the other guy that stopped every April at the IRS tollbooth.

Avoiding the tollbooth is one picture that explains tax-deferral and there are many more. I used to use a picture of two buckets, one with a hole in it and another with a spigot – the tag line was that tax-deferral avoids having the IRS punch a hole in your financial bucket to drain off cash, but instead gives you a faucet so that you control when the IRS gets paid.

The point is we remember pictures better than we remember graphs and math tables, and by making our rational point with a picture the consumer is more likely to remember the point. It is also easier to explain the reason for the purchase is because the annuity provides an IRS Easy-Pass rather than saying "assuming a 25% tax rate the annuity has a tax-equivalent rate of y."

<u>Specific Dollars</u>

We talk about tax deferral like it is something separate and distinct, but it is not. Taxes are a cost on the yield and nothing more. It is usually better to pay a dollar of taxes tomorrow rather than today – you can earn interest on the money that would have gone for taxes – which is why tax deferral can effectively increase yields, but it is still a matter of dollars and cents. Tax deferral can be a negative for someone that will be in a much higher tax rate when the interest is received and a positive if the tax rate is a lower or the same down the road.

If you want to get across the benefit of tax-deferral show how it impacts the buyer:

Ask to see a copy of last year's Form 1040 so that you can go to line 8a and show them their taxable interest income will be reduced from X to Y.

Flip over the Form 1040 so you can show that "the $2,000 that is now tax-deferred interest will lower your tax bill by $500.

Counter a worry about a future tax obligation with hard dollars, "assuming your tax bracket stays the same even if you cash out the multi-year annuity in five years you will still have $1280 more in your pocket than you would have netted with the five year CD."

Calculate whether deferred interest can reduce or eliminate any Social Security benefit taxation.

And talk about tax control. No longer does the bank or bond issuer tell you when you have to pay taxes on interest you are not spending. With a deferred annuity you are once again in charge.

Tax Deferral In Qualified Plans
    Annuity interest grows tax-deferred. Money in qualified plans grows tax-deferred. A fixed annuity inside a qualified plan is already growing tax-deferred, which leads some people to say a

24

fixed annuity should not be used in a qualified plan. This assumes the main reason one buys a fixed annuity is for tax-deferral; however, my research suggests people buy a fixed annuity primarily for the potentially higher yield in a safe place.

If your IRA choice was a fixed annuity yielding 6% or a similar non-tax-deferred vehicle yielding 5%, which one would you pick? The decision to buy a fixed annuity is primarily based on return, not tax benefits.

To Be Guaranteed You Will Always Earn Something
A fixed annuity means you will always earn at least some interest each year in the future even if interest rates drop (although the guarantee may be a tiny amount of interest that is credited retroactively in the case of many index annuities). This means fixed annuities may offer more competitive yields over the long haul than other fixed interest vehicles even in times of very low interest rates.

Fixed Annuity Interest

The only other no-market-risk to principal savings place that has a minimum interest guarantee is a Savings Bond. I Bonds guarantee a fixed rate of interest plus interest based on changes in the Consumer Price Index – as I am writing this the current fixed rate is zero. Series EE Bonds guarantee to return double your principal if you hold them for 20 years – an effective return of 3.5% – but if you take out your money early you earned the locked in rate – which as I write this is 1.4%. In actual dollars this means if you put $5000 into a Series EE Bond in 2008 you would get back $10,000 in 20 years, <u>but</u> if you cashed in the annuity in 19 years and 364 days you would get back $6,602; this is equivalent to <u>a 68% savings bond surrender charge!</u>

Fixed annuities provide a minimum guaranteed interest rate. If the insurance company believes it can pay extra interest from their general account, above and beyond this minimum guarantee, they will declare a fixed rate of interest and pay the annuity owner a stated interest rate for a period, or, in the case of index annuities they will declare a stated participation rate for the period.

To Receive An Income You Cannot Outlive
Only an annuity can provide an income that is guaranteed to last a lifetime. The effective yield received by annuitization increases the longer one lives.

Ask the consumer "When are you going to die?" When no answer follows mention that Wall Street's answers to retirement income are the "pick and pray" kind in that you pick a withdrawal rate and pray you do not die before the money runs out.

With annuities you can guarantee an income for as long as you live and you have choices on how to do this. You can maximize the income by annuitization and this allows you to receive income for as long as you live, or as long you and your spouse lives. The other way to use annuities is to choose one with Guaranteed Lifetime Withdrawal Benefits (GLWBs). The GLWB pays a lower income than annuitization, but you retain control of the principal

GLWBs

I cannot tell you what the stock market will do tomorrow, but I can tell you if you put money into any number of annuities offering Guaranteed Lifetime Withdrawal Benefits (GLWBs) you will know the minimum annual lifetime payout you will receive at a future date regardless of what the stock market or interest rates do.

Fixed annuities have always been able to predict the future thru minimum guarantees, but the future was minimal. If at age 50 you placed $100,000 in an annuity with a 3% interest guarantee – a strong rate today – a cursory look at current life annuitization rates says that resulting balance would generate a lifelong income of around $13,000 a year at age 65, but you would lose control of the asset. Several annuities with GLWBs would guarantee $15,000 in lifetime income under this scenario and you still keep control of the asset.

If the goal is to provide income for life and control of the asset, annuity GLWBs are looking more and more as the better solution to taking out a miserly safe rate from a portfolio and crossing your fingers, or converting and losing assets to build an income stream. With a little planning annuity GLWBs are available that may offer significantly higher payouts than past attempts at providing a lasting retirement income.

Because Losses Hurt

If you have $1 and you lose 20 cents of that dollar, what percentage increase is needed to bring the remaining 80 cents back to a dollar? Although the answer might appear to be 20%, the real answer is you need a 25% increase to regain what you have lost. In a bear market some investments lost 50% of their value; this means those investments need to increase 100% to merely get back to where they were.

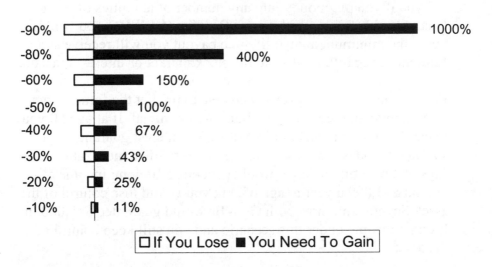

Loss Hurts

If You Lose	You Need To Gain
-90%	1000%
-80%	400%
-60%	150%
-50%	100%
-40%	67%
-30%	43%
-20%	25%
-10%	11%

☐ If You Lose ■ You Need To Gain

Another Example

Let us say you had an investment that had four strong up years and one bad down year and compared it to an annuity where you only earned half of what the investment return is in the up years but you did not lose money in the down year. If you put $10,000 into each, which one was worth more at the end of 5 years?

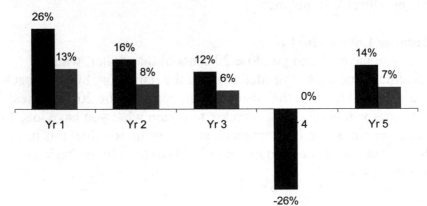

	Yr 1	Yr 2	Yr 3	4	Yr 5
	26%	16%	12%	-26%	14%
	13%	8%	6%	0%	7%

The annuity wins ($13,842 versus $13,810 for the investment). These numbers are cherry-picked so the annuity would win – if you want the investment to win read a different book – but the main point is even infrequent losses can severely impact gains.

As another example, if you earned 10% for 4 years and then had a 9% loss in year 5, you are worse off than if you had simply earned 6% for all five years.

To Avoid Probate

An annuity is a life insurance contract; therefore proceeds are distributed to named beneficiaries under the terms of the contract and bypass probate. A fixed annuity can help a consumer avoid probate, which can help reduce or eliminate fees that would lower returns. However, it is simple to avoid probate on other assets too by using things like joint tenancy, Payable On Death set ups, or living trusts.

To Avoid Risk

The twin topics of risk and safety are so important to the typical annuitybuyer that the entire next chapter talks about annuity safety. However, we can talk about risk and return in a purely economic way. From a rational economic viewpoint all financial decisions are made on a risk/return continuum or scale. The rational consumer is always trying to earn the highest possible return for a given level of risk.

Defining return is relatively easy. The return is what remains in your pocket after all costs – including tax considerations – are taken care of. Whatever is left is the return.

Risk is more difficult to define because there are different types of risk. There is inflation risk – the purchasing power lost due to higher prices, and diversification risk – having all your eggs in one basket and dropping the basket, even catastrophic risk – being financially wiped out by a cataclysmic event like a hurricane. Most people I have talked with think about financial risk as losing the money they have – the original money or principal they put in and the return they have received thus far. It is this context that we will talk about economic risk.

Classical economic theory answers the question "How do you get a higher return?" with "Accept a higher level of risk." Do you want lower risk? Accept a lower return. Although there are times when a vehicle's return may be higher or lower than its actual risk level, the returns are soon adjusted so that the universe returns to financial harmony.

So, in the rational world a consumer will buy a fixed annuity because they are willing to assume the risk level for the potential return, and unwilling to accept the higher risk of another vehicle to get a higher return – a very neat and rational positioning of the fixed annuity solution.

Risk Tolerance
Risk does differ based on income and sex. The higher the income, generally the higher the risk tolerance, and men have a higher risk tolerance than women. However, risk tolerance cannot be predicted by Age, Marital Status, or Education. What this means in the annuity world is a 75 year old may have a higher risk tolerance than a 45 year old and it means the suitability of a fixed annuity purchase is not based on age but on the risk aversion of the consumer.

Blatant Benefits of Fixed Annuities

Modesty may be a fine quality, but it is at odds with the marketing of annuities. With all the noise created by purveyors of other financial products an annuity provider cannot be soft-spoken in relaying the benefits of buying one. You need to state annuity benefits loud and clear.

Do not simply say *Tax Deferral*, instead SHOUT – **Fixed annuities give you control over when you pay taxes on your interest.**

Do not simply say *Multiple year interest guarantee*, instead SHOUT – **Fixed annuities offers protection against interest rate uncertainty.**

Do not simply say *Minimum Guarantee*, instead SHOUT – **Fixed annuities guarantee to pay you a return for as long as you choose to own one.**

Do not simply say *Protected from market risk*, instead SHOUT – **No fixed annuity owner has ever lost a dime due to a stock market downturn.**

Do not simply say *Safe*, instead SHOUT – **No index annuity owner has ever lost a dime because a carrier failed.**

And Claim The Obvious Benefit

Bayer® Aspirin advertises it has an ingredient that will help protect people from heart attacks. The ingredient is called aspirin and at my local drugstore it costs 8 cents a tablet for Bayer brand Aspirin. The drugstore also sells generic aspirin at less than 1 cent a tablet. Bayer sells over half a billion dollars a year of a product that is available in generic form that provides the same identical benefit for heart attacks for a fraction of the cost. But the benefit claimed is BAYER aspirin helps to prevent heart attacks.

Everyone in sales tries to gain a competitive advantage where a benefit can be touted that is unique to the seller. However, the advantage is not gained thru actual benefit exclusivity but thru the perception of exclusivity, and this can be accomplished by loudly and frequently claiming the obvious benefit as ones own.

For example, all deferred annuities offer tax-deferral of compounding interest, and this is often stated as a benefit of

31

owning an annuity. This does not mean a seller cannot run a full page ad stating, "MY COMPANY gives you *FREE Tax-Deferral* of compounding interest."

Or, there is nothing to stop a representative from saying about the annuities represented that "MY ANNUITIES will pay out your annuity death benefit directly to your beneficiary giving you the ability to *avoid probate at no additional charge*"

A feature common to all annuities is the ability to annuitize to receive a life income, but this could also be expressed as "MY COMPANY *Will Put It In Writing* that you can have *an income for as long as you live.*" While another annuity benefit that can be claimed is "THIS ANNUITY *protects principal* from stock market loss" with a strong emphasis on "THIS."

The benefit claimed does not even need to be directly associated with the product as long as claiming it creates a positive perception. Saying "Every one of OUR COMPANY Employees Has A Mother" or "MY COMPANY does not club baby seals" sounds silly, but then you start to wonder about why other companies are not making these claims.

Claiming benefits is by no means a unique idea; the marketing world is full of attempts at branding the obvious, because it works. Annuity carriers and representatives can be more effective by talking about what "MY ANNUITY offers" and claiming these benefits.

Marketing is finding people that may need the solution you offer. In today's crowded world you may only get one chance to be heard, so make it strong.

Take A General Benefit And Make It Specific
You could market Acme Car Wax by saying it is durable, but it is more effective to say *"Acme Car Wax protects your Lexus finish for 12 months."* As consumers we want solutions to *our* problem

not *the* problem, and we want to be *talked with* not *talked at*. This means do not talk in generalities, but make it specific to the consumer. Some examples:

"Do you want to earn 2 types or 3 types of interest on your money?"

This plays to our greedy side because we usually want more. The three types of interest are interest on your principal (simple interest), interest on your interest (compound interest), and interest on your deferred taxes (tax control interest).

"Would you rather your $50,000 become $100,000 in 12 years or 18 years?"

This uses the Rule of 72 assuming 6% interest and a 33% tax rate so 2% is lost to taxes. In an annuity the money doubles in 12 year [72/6%] but it takes 18 years sitting in a taxable account [72/(6%-2%)]. Use the actual amount of money being considered for the annuity purchase.

"By earning that $4,000 in interest in the annuity instead of the bank you could save enough in taxes to pay for that needed life insurance policy...your property taxes...groceries"

For someone at a 25% tax rate moving $100,000 from a CD to a deferred annuity could save $1000 in current annual taxes – even when they both yield 4%. The thousand bucks is real money and can be used to pay for real needs.

"Could you use an extra $3,000? Based on (the current rate or current index cap) this annuity gives you the potential for $3,000 more interest than where you are now"

We tend to talk in terms of percents – and this still makes sense because 5% is greater than 4% which is greater than 2% – and we respond to bigger, but percents are an abstract concept. Show the annuity benefit to the consumer. Saying "the extra interest this annuity earns will pay your light bill or cover a new car payment" the consumer understands why the benefit is needed.

<u>Other Specific Benefits</u>

> *"You will not lose your $75,000 nest egg*
> *if the stock market goes down"*

> *"When you die your spouse will receive only half or less of*
> *your current Social Security benefit; the lifetime income from*
> *this annuity would replace that lost income"*

> *"Because this annuity will not go through probate your son*
> *will not know how much money you left your daughter"*

Talking About Surrender Charges

The number one complaint to regulators year after year is from annuitybuyers saying they did not realize the length and severity of the surrender charge. Based on my experience, consumer complaints are often the result of selective listening – the representative did cover both the good and bad points but the consumer only remembered the good; however, they also result from some representatives doing a circuitous presentation dance when disclosing the charges that limit access to the annuityowner's money.

The consumer must know what it will cost to get out of the contract on any given day and understand exactly what the surrender charge is and when it is applied. However, I have a problem with the phrase "surrender charge" because it is not truly accurate. It sounds like a charge against all annuity owners, but who actually pays the charge?

Do you pay this charge if you keep the annuity? No.

Do you pay this charge if you withdraw the annual interest credited? Typically not, most annuities permit an annual 10% withdrawal beginning on the 366th day of annuity ownership without incurring a surrender charge.

Do you pay this charge if you die? Typically not, and even annuities that do not waive surrender charges at death usually offer a way to get around them by delaying the payout.

Do you pay this charge for as long as you own the annuity? Typically not, unlike a certificate of deposit that restarts its penalties with each new interest period, the annuity charge usually ends at some specified point in the future.

I prefer to look at these charges as temporary and voluntary liquidity costs, with the realization that all financial instruments have liquidity costs.

Whether the first-year surrender penalty is 5% or 15%, the consumer only pays the penalty if they cash in the policy. The real question is what was the alternative to buying the annuity?

If an index annuity credits 12% the first year, has a 10% surrender charge, and the money market account the annuity funds came from pays 1%, which instrument has cost the consumer the most if cashed in at the end of one year? The answer is the money market because the annuity nets the consumer 2% if cashed in whole the money market nets 1%.

The consumer always needs to know the liquidity costs. Perhaps a better way for the representative to explain liquidity cost is to compare the real net results of the annuity with the alternative.

An Annuity Magic Act

<u>How To Compare An Annuity With An Investment</u>

Buy an inflatable punching clown – the one with a weighted bottom that bounces back up after you hit it – and paint the words "market risk" on it. Also buy two plastic baseball bats and label one "investment"" and one "fixed annuity"

Hit the clown with the investment bat and as it rises each time explain how with investments even when you think you have market risk under control it is always ready to rise up and confront you again. Then hit the clown with the fixed annuity bat. The clown will stay down and you can show how fixed annuities K.O. market risk. *(The secret is the fixed annuity bat has a nail in it that punctures the clown)*.

<u>The Effect Of Minimum Guaranteed Interest</u>

Wrap up a bit of baking soda in two tissues and tie a string to it. Half-fill two test tubes with liquid each containing a baking soda

36

bag hanging slightly above the surface of the liquid, and then snap a balloon over the top of the test tube so you have an airtight seal. Explain that there is a big difference between CD interest and fixed annuity interest. Shake the first test tube and the balloon doesn't inflate – explain this represents there are no guarantees on the interest you may earn in the future on a CD, and it could even be zero interest in any given year. Shake the second test tube and the balloon inflates – explain that fixed annuities always guarantee you'll earn at least the guaranteed interest each year regardless of what the future holds. (*The secret is the CD tube contains water but the annuity tube holds white vinegar*).

Tax Deferral Protection

Show how fixed annuities can protect your interest earnings from taxes. Build two stacks of sugar cubes and place one stack under plastic wrap. Fill a small watering can and as you are pouring it over the stacks of sugar cubes explain that the water represents the torrent of taxation that can wash away your interest. However, fixed annuities are protected by a shield of tax deferral that keeps your interest intact until you decide to spend it. (*The secret is the plastic wrap keeps the water from dissolving the sugar*).

***Protection from market risk, tax deferral, minimum guarantees –
Is it magic or a fixed annuity***

Annuities – How Much Is Too Much?

I have been asked by several people what percentage of a consumer's assets should be in annuities. Is there a percentage that is too high or too low? Does the correct percentage vary by age? Should it be higher or lower depending on your total assets?

My answer to them has been that I do not know; I do not believe you can plug some factoids into some model and figure out what percentage of an individual's assets should be in annuities, because it is not simply an economic decision.

Should a person have no more than 60% of their total assets in annuities? Possibly, if their risk tolerance was low and they might need, say, an additional 6% of the annuity value to meet possibly liquidity needs (most fixed annuities offer 10% annual withdrawal without penalties assessed).

What about putting 90% of the money in annuities? If a consumer had a million dollars and an overriding goal of leaving at least $900,000 to heirs the annuities could protect the legacy from market risk and still provide access to a lot of penalty-free cash.

Is 1% too much? It could be if all of the assets might be needed within the year, or if the consumer has such a bugaboo about liquidity constraints that they only buy airline tickets while boarding the plane.

I view a fixed annuity as a safe money place protecting principal and credited interest from market risk. I believe the first question a consumer needs to answer is how much of their money should be in safe money places and how much in risk money places, and I believe the answer comes down to how the consumer feels about risk of loss. For me, that is a personal question and the "correct" answer will differ from person to person.

Let us say a consumer does decide that 50% of their money should be safe, how much of that should be in fixed annuities? That would depend primarily on liquidity needs. Often – but definitely not always – safe money instruments with longer penalties pay higher yields than those without penalties. The reason why is usually because the issuer knows they have the money to work with a little longer so they can afford to pay a little more interest.

Fixed annuities have liquidity penalties that typically range from 1 to 15 years. If you think you would need all of the money in 5 years, it would not make sense to buy an annuity with 10 years of penalties. But what if the odds were you would not need the money in 5 years or even 20 years? Then the annuity might be the best place for a chunk of the safe money.

The questions that need to be answered are how does the consumer feel about market risk and what are the liquidity needs of the consumer. The "correct" answer will vary from consumer to consumer.

Rationally, Who Is A Fixed Annuity Candidate

Let us examine who is a fixed annuity prospect from a rational perspective.

Not A Candidate

Who is not a fixed annuity candidate? In broad terms, if someone has a high risk tolerance and wants the highest return they would buy an investment – stocks, mutual funds, hard assets. These investors are not fixed annuity candidates.

At the other extreme are consumers that have accounts at five different banks to ensure all deposits stay with FDIC coverage limits. There are consumers that would not buy a U.S. Treasury bill because it is not FDIC insured. And, let us face it, there are consumers that are FDIC groupies and will never buy a fixed annuity.

So everyone else is a fixed annuity prospect. However, that definition is so broad as to be meaningless. Let us really look at who are potential fixed annuity buyers.

Weak Candidates

An investor is probably not going to switch from stocks to fixed annuities – unless they should never have been a stock buyer in the first place. However, investors may use a fixed annuity for their lower risk investment money – as an example they may use fixed annuities instead of bonds – but I have found it is difficult to break across the "stocks & bonds" mentality that many investors (and financial counselors) have, even though a strong case can be made to use fixed annuities instead of bond funds. Bonds react to market forces and can gain and lose value, so that even a bond mutual fund that is very low risk from a credit risk standpoint can still go down in value due to interest rate risk.

Strong Candidates

The ideal candidate is the consumer that will accept the very slightly higher credit risk of the fixed annuity because of the higher potential return, but does not want market risk. This consumer merely needs to be asked which fixed annuity they wish to purchase.

The number of strong prospects increases as the spread between bank rates and fixed annuity yield – or potential yields – increases. When bank rates are falling and annuity rates are holding people move into the fixed annuity arena, but when bank rates are rising the bank seems like a very good place to be.

Everybody Else

Misplaced investors are fixed annuity prospects. In the last couple bull markets many savers entered the stock market because they perceived the market risk to be lower than its actual risk level. When the stock market returns were "adjusted" by the subsequent bear market many of these investors became stock market refugees. Many returned to the bank, but some were led to the fixed annuity shore.

A fixed annuity has the potential for a little higher yield than a certificate of deposit at a very slight increase in risk (as we define risk). Market risk does not affect principal and credited interest, and the risk of issuer default has historically been comparable with banks.

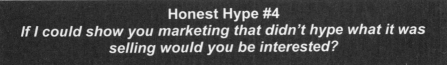

Honest Hype #4
If I could show you marketing that didn't hype what it was selling would you be interested?

Annuities offer real advantages that do not need to be hyped.

Sales Points

➤ Consumers are often not even aware of what annuities can do for them so they are not even a part of the financial decision process

➤ We do not like to change decisions because that may force us to admit we made a mistake, but we can make a different decision today without admitting the mistake by believing circumstances have changed and today is different

➤ Listen to the consumer explain why they do not like annuities so that you can provide the reason the consumer was right not to buy yesterday but will be right to buy the annuity today

➤ Annuities – whether fixed rate or index – have proven they provide potentially higher yields than bank CDs and can be competitive with taxable bond funds

➤ Tax Deferral means you do not have to stop at the IRA tollbooth each year

Background Sources

Simon, Herbert. 1997. *Administrative Behavior, 4th Edition*. New York. The Free Press. 92-139

Chapter 3 – Safety

There are different levels of risk (or different levels of safety if you wish to look at it from the other direction) associated with fixed annuities. There is inflation risk where decreasing purchasing power makes today's money worth less tomorrow. There is tax risk where you pay taxes you did not need to pay. Longevity risk is outliving your money. And there is currency risk, political risk, legal risk, benefit shortfall risk, and if given enough time we could probably think of many more (annuity envy risk?). However, I find when most people think of risk they think about the risk of losing their principal. Safety is such a strong issue in an annuity sale that I have devoted an entire chapter to it. The early part of the chapter is supposed to give the representative a better understanding of the safety issues in an annuity and how it all affects the interest paid to the annuityowner. The last part contains data points and third party references you can give to a consumer to help them feel more comfortable about buying an annuity.

Fixed Annuity Risk

Investments have market risk meaning if the market price goes down for the investment you are holding you could lose money if you sold. The market risk of stocks, bonds, commodities, collectibles, real estate, gold, oil and even variable annuities is the value of the asset could go down – perhaps to zero – if the market was unfavorable. Fixed annuities do not expose principal and credited interest to market risk, although you could argue that potential interest is subject to a type of market risk.

Three fixed annuity risks are return risk, liquidity risk and capital risk

Credit or capital risk is another matter. What happens if the insurance company backing the fixed annuity cannot pay? What this chapter is about are the three risks I get the most questions about:

- Return risk – not earning a fair return on your money.

- Liquidity risk – not being able to get your money when you want it or not getting the money you thought you were going to get.

- Capital risk – losing your money because the insurer goes bust.

Let us look at what affects these different risks and how concerned we should be.

Return Risk

Carrier Investments

One of the reasons that so few life and annuity carriers have failed is because the state insurance departments regulate the type of investments carriers may use and limit the amount of assets that may be used in riskier investments. What this means is the bulk of the assets are usually placed in investment grade bonds, and only a smattering of the assets are placed in stocks, real estate and below investment grade (junk) bonds.

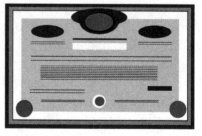

This does not mean a carrier that is invested entirely in government bonds is safer than one that is not. A couple other factors that matter are the yields earned on the bonds and the maturity of the bond portfolio (a primer on how interest rates affect bonds is in the back of the chapter).

Bond Yields

Typically, the lower the risk that the bond issuer will default on paying on the bond the lower is the yield on the bond. It is the old risk versus return equation where lower risk translates into lower returns. If a carrier buys nothing but U.S. government bonds they know the interest will be paid and the face value will be there at maturity, and this is why the yields on these bonds are low. As the risk of bond issuer defaults increases a higher yield is demanded by bond buyers. A riskier corporate bond may pay 2%, 4%, or 8% more than a government bond and would allow the carrier to pay higher rates on their annuities, but what happens if the riskier bond quits paying?

An insurance carrier tries to find a balance that provides the highest overall yield with the lowest risk of bond defaults. Investing too heavily in junk bonds could mean losses if the bonds live up to their name. At the other end, buying only government bonds may mean there is not enough yield to provide a competitive return.

Bond Maturity Length

If you hold a bond until maturity the issuer will pay back the face value of the bond – a bond with a face value of $1000 will return $1000 when the bond matures. Usually the longer the maturity of the bond the greater the yield, so it would seem to make sense to buy bonds with the longest term to get the highest yield. However, what if someone cashes in the annuity before the bond matures? If bond rates have been heading up the carrier may not get the face value of the bond if it sells before maturity.

The carrier usually tries to match up the portfolio bond maturity length with how long the annuity policies are expected to stay on the books, because they do not want to get caught with annuityowners cashing in policies early forcing the carriers to sell bonds below their maturity value. What this means is a carrier with a book of in-force annuities with 5-year surrender periods would usually buy shorter maturity bonds than if the book consisted of annuities with 10-year surrender periods. Since shorter maturity bonds typically yield less than longer maturity ones the 5-year annuities should pay lower yields than the 10-year annuities. It also means the annuity carrier will try to discourage annuityowners from cashing in early by charging surrender penalties.

Costs

The lower the costs, the greater the available return to the annuityowner. If one carrier spends less than another on operating the business year after year there is more money available to pay the annuityowner. There are also acquisition costs in getting the consumer to buy the annuity, and these include marketing dollars, agent and marketing organization commissions, and bonuses. These upfront costs are amortized over the expected life of the annuity and reduce the annual return to the annuityowner.

Index Annuity Option Costs

Most index annuity carriers buy options to allow annuityowners to benefit from increases in the index calculation. If the carrier had enough remaining cash after subtracting costs from the yield realized on the bonds backing an annuity to buy an option covering the entire annuity value, the annuityowner could realize 100% of any increase in the value of that option. However, if the carrier can only buy 60% of the option with the available money the annuityowner participates in 60% of the calculated growth in the value of the option. Who gets the other 40%? The option seller gets the 40%; not the insurance company.

The typical carrier makes money on the spread between what the carrier portfolio yields and what is paid to the annuityowner. With index annuities the carrier typically buys an option from an option seller using money that would normally be paid out as interest in a fixed rate annuity. In other words, if the carrier had a nickel of yield left over for each dollar of annuity premium the carrier would declare a 5% interest rate if these were fixed rate annuities. If they were index annuities the carrier would use the nickel to buy index options and the annuityowner would hope the value of the option rose more than 5% by the end of the period.

The carrier does not usually want to be at risk for paying the annuityowner the potential upside of the index-linked interest so they hedge this risk by finding an option seller that will cover some predetermined percentage of the possible upside. What happens if the index goes up? The option seller pays the carrier the index-linked gain they are entitled to and the carrier credits this interest to the annuity policy. What if the index goes down? The option seller will use the nickel they got from the carrier to help offset their losses, the annuity policy does not earn index-linked interest, and the carrier is unaffected.

Although most carriers simply buy options to hedge or cover any exposure for index-linked interest a few companies use *dynamic hedging* where the carrier creates a model of the index using a combination of investments. The advantage is this may be less expensive for the carrier than buying the actual options, but the disadvantage is if the carrier screws up they could be on the hook for more money.

What matters to the annuityowner is the yield they see on their annuity statement. The real answer why the consumer may not get all of the index upside is because they chose a financial instrument that protects them from market risk on the downside and it cost the carrier to provide this protection. The consumer cannot have it both ways.

A Premium Bonus Is Not Free
It is nice to tell a consumer they will receive an extra 5% or 10% bonus added to their annuity premium if they select a particular annuity. However, would the consumer be as receptive if they were also told that this bonus is essentially prepaid interest, meaning they will earn less in subsequent years than if they had picked an identical annuity without a bonus? There are bonuses ranging from 1% to as high as 12%, but regardless of the size the reality is the cost of these upfront bonuses will all be deducted out of future interest earnings.

A bonus is a cost to the contract, just like commissions and policy expenses. These costs are amortized over the expected life of the contract. The higher the costs, the greater the annual expense deducted from the gross interest earned. If you are comparing two annuity contracts that are identical, except that one has an upfront bonus and the other does not, the one with the bonus will earn less interest at future renewal periods.

Bonus Math

Suppose you have three annuities: one has no bonus and a 10-year surrender period, the second has a 10% bonus and a 10-year surrender period, and the third has a 10% bonus and a 20-year surrender period. If the annuities have the same commission and pricing, what would the client get at renewal if the net available to the contract after expenses was 5%?

The first annuity would earn 5%.

The second annuity would need to recapture the bonus over the 10-year surrender period. A 10% bonus divided by 10 years means 1% would need to be recaptured each year from renewal rates so the second annuity would earn 5% minus 1% or 4%.

The third annuity would need to recapture the bonus over the 20-year surrender period. A 10% bonus divided by 20 years means 0.5% would need to be recaptured each year from renewal rates so the second annuity would earn 5% minus 0.5% or 4.5%.

Does this mean an upfront bonus is bad? Not necessarily. A consumer may prefer to have a "bird in the hand" in the shape of a tangible bonus today rather than trust those bonus bucks to the future uncertainties of the financial markets. An index annuity with an upfront bonus may be better positioned to take advantage of up periods in the early years of the policy and maybe earn more index-linked interest than they would without an initial bonus. However, a problem can arise if the realities of the bonus are not fully explained when transfers from existing annuity contracts are involved and the existing contracts have surrender charges that the bonus is considered to be "covering."

Say that an existing contract has a remaining surrender penalty period of five years and a transfer to a new contract will result in a 7% surrender charge on the existing one. If the new contract has a 10% bonus at first blush it might appear that a transfer to the new annuity would pay off the old 7% charge and leave the consumer with 3% found money. However, the cost of that 10% bonus is amortized and deducted from future earnings. In essence, not only does the consumer still feel the effect of the old 7% surrender charge, but also the effect will impact future earnings longer than the 5 years left originally.

All of this does not mean that it is bad to do an exchange from an existing policy to a new annuity that pays an upfront bonus. What it means is there should be other solid financial reasons for making the exchange, which might include a stronger minimum guarantee on the new policy, or perhaps the new policy offers additional ways of earning interest (index-linked interest or guaranteed living benefits for example). But even these reasons may not be enough if the old policy still had surrender charges. In that case, the customer must be made to understand that he or she is funding that part of the bonus that compensated for the surrender charges.

Renewal Rates
Two companies offer a fixed annuity. Each annuity has the same initial rate, the same minimum guarantee, the same surrender charges and surrender term, the same withdrawal features and riders, and identical representative and override commissions. The products are identical. Will they also offer identical renewal rates in future years? It is unlikely.

There are two renewal philosophies; the first is *portfolio rate* where the net carrier portfolio yield is allocated equally to the annuities. This would be where one annuity was purchased four years ago and the same annuity product was purchased one year ago and both products would renew at the same rate. The second renewal philosophy is *banded rate* where the carrier internally treats the annuity premiums as if they have their own personal portfolio based on the assets bought when the annuity is purchased. With a banded rate method the carrier would see what the net yield was on the assets purchased four years ago, and then pay based on the net yield for this annuity, and then the carrier would look at the bonds purchased one year ago and credit a renewal rate based on the net yield of those specific assets for that annuity.

Only 2 out of 25 carriers used a portfolio rate renewal strategy

Most representatives I have talked with believe the fixed annuities they sell use the portfolio rate method where everyone receives the same renewal rate regardless when the product was purchased (and most carrier wholesalers told me the same thing). However, a couple of years ago when I asked the 25 largest fixed annuity carriers whether they use a portfolio rate or banded rate strategy and only 2 said they used a portfolio rate renewal!

What does this all mean? With a portfolio rate method newer annuities will be penalized in a rising interest rate environment because the lower rates on the older bonds within the carrier portfolio will be holding down the current market interest rates. With a banded rate renewal philosophy newer annuities would receive higher rates in a rising interest rate environment but older annuities purchased when rates were lower would continue to receive lower renewal rates.

The banded rate method makes more sense to me because each product has its own pricing elements. An annuity with a higher initial commission has fewer dollars available to buy bonds and so will always have a lower renewal rate than a comparable product with a lower commission, or an annuity with a 10 year surrender period will have different bond maturities than an annuity with a 5 year surrender period, and the renewal rate will show this.

I typically hear complaints on the carriers using banded rate when rates are rising and new annuities have higher rates than existing annuities (but I never hear complaints when rates are falling).

Regulatory financial requirements mean most of the money in a carrier's investment portfolio is in bonds, but as discussed, a carrier can alter the quality and average maturity of their bond portfolio to lean towards higher yield or lower risk. A carrier can play it conservative and put most of the money in high grade bonds and accept a lower yield, or they can attempt to increase the yield by including more high-yield bonds and hope that through good management and a bit of luck that the extra yield they receive will not be taken away by bonds going bad.

Index annuities have a different set of factors that will affect their renewal rates. The typical carrier buys options to provide the index-linked interest potential. If exchange listed options (existing options traded on stock exchanges) can be used the costs may be lower than if synthetic options are created by the option seller and bought by the carrier. Lower option costs means more options may be purchased for each dollar of premium, which translates into higher caps or participation rates. In addition, big option buyers get quantity pricing breaks. A carrier buying $25 million of options usually gets a better price than another buying $1 million of options, which means the big buyer gets more options for each dollar spent and this can translate into higher caps or rates. And, a carrier might forgo buying any options by using dynamic hedging.

But whether the bonds are "AAA" or "BB" and their maturity is 10 years or 25 years, or whether the index link is produced by exchange traded options, over-the-counter options, or dynamic hedging, it is the carrier that sets the renewal rate. Carriers make pricing assumptions on policy expenses that may be more conservative or less conservative, and these assumptions affect how much money is available for renewal rates. One carrier may require a 14% return on their equity while another is happy earning a 12% return (and less money taken by the carrier leaves more money for the annuityowner). And renewal rates are set by people, which means their decisions may have emotional factors at play that are not backed by economic factors. All of these different factors determine annuity renewal rates.

Index Annuities Returns – What Can Go Wrong?

Many years ago I worked for an investment banking firm. Shortly after I joined the firm I was invited to participate in a meeting where our finance people and attorneys were all sitting at a table trying to figure out the proper risk disclosure language for the prospectus of a new offering the firm was trying to underwrite. The product offering was fat in fees and the company would make a lot of money. The problem was that unless a very precise set of unlikely economic circumstances came to pass, the investors would probably lose their money.

There was a lot of banter back and forth about the proper tone the disclosure language should take, so that the firm would be protected and there would still be some sizzle on the marketing steak, but it was tough to strike the balance. Finally, they asked for my opinion. I said we should state in bold letters "investors in this offering will probably lose their investment, but they might not." My suggestion was not adopted and I never got invited back to another meeting.

My position has always been that consumers are fully responsible for the consequences of what they are buying as long as the risks are disclosed. I further believe consumers will still buy a product, even after all the risks are disclosed, if the product fits their needs. An index annuity provides protection of principal and credited interest from market risk. An index annuity also provides a shot at making more than the guaranteed minimum rate of interest. Okay, what are the risks that should be disclosed?

Index Annuities – What Can Go Wrong?

- Stock Market can be flat or go down for a prolonged period so only minimum interest is earned

- Unforeseen Political and economic developments negatively affect the value of stocks in the index and thereby lower the value of the index so only minimum interest is earned

- Bond Yields can be so low few options can be bought so index annuity participation stinks

- Option Prices can be so high few options can be bought so index annuity participation stinks

- Economics are fine, but management decides to increase carrier profits by cutting renewal rates

- Economics are fine, but carrier pricing people did not hedge index annuity properly so renewal rates stay at guaranteed minimum for years

- Insurance Company can go out of business

- This List does not cover everything and something else goes wrong

Another disclosure is often needed when the topic of minimum interest is raised. With very few exceptions minimum interest is usually not credited until the end of the surrender period, and is only credited if index-linked interest is insufficient. Furthermore, many policies base the crediting on less than 100% of the premium meaning that actual interest paid is less than the apparent interest rate.

If the representative does not provide full disclosure, an unhappy annuity buyer may not understand why zero interest was credited in contract year 4, and why the table in the policy shows an effective minimum interest rate of 1.92% a year instead of 3.00%. One way to provide full disclosure is to talk about minimum return and not minimum interest. It would be saying something along the lines of "Although the minimum interest is not credited each year, the annuityowner receives a minimum return of at least 20.95% at the end of ten years" or whatever the minimum return is.

Different index annuity crediting methods require accurate disclosures of risks. Averaging needs to be presented as "driving values to the middle" instead of "smoothes out the low points." Caps need to be explained as the maximum that can be earned instead of the probable return. A rate highlighted as "guaranteed for the term" does not mean "but the carrier can change the spread or cap each year."

A good index annuity protects principal and credited interest from market risk while providing the potential for a higher interest rate than might be earned on other savings vehicles. An index annuity is not perfect, but even with all the risks disclosed it is an excellent financial tool. If full disclosure is made and the consumer does not choose an index annuity, it probably did not meet their needs.

Liquidity Risk

Surrender Charges

Most, but not all, fixed annuities have penalties for early liquidity. I have seen penalties last from one year to forever – these are the two-tier annuities that always impose a penalty unless the account value is annuitized. Before I dig further into surrender penalties let us look at the liquidity that is typically not penalized.

Annual withdrawals – Most deferred annuities permit 10% of the account value to be withdrawn each year after beginning the second year of the contract. A few allow cumulative withdrawals so whatever free withdrawal not used one year may be used the next year or the year after that. Fewer annuities allow free withdrawals during the first contract year. Fewer still restrict the withdrawal percentage to 5% of account value and almost no one bans all free withdrawals. The "free" means a surrender penalty or account value adjustment is not imposed; it has nothing to do with possible tax consequences.

Death Benefit – Few deferred annuities place a surrender charge or require annuitization upon death of the annuity owner.

Nursing Home/Hospitalization/Unemployment/Etc. – Some deferred annuities waive surrender charges if certain events occur – like being confined to a nursing home.

Surrender Charges And Bonus

A while back some media folks were making noise about one annuity that imposed a 20% penalty if the contract was surrendered. However, the annuity credited an upfront 10% premium bonus so the net effect if the annuity was surrendered in the first year was that the annuityowner got back 90% of the premium for an effective liquidity charge of 10%.

Often the reason for a high surrender percentage is to recapture the bonus credited. To keep the initial penalties lower some companies credit an upfront bonus that vests over time, so if you were to surrender your 10 year surrender schedule annuity paying a 10% premium bonus in 5 years you might only get to keep 5% of the bonus.

Surrender Charges And Commissions

The *yield curve* usually rewards longer maturity bonds with higher yields. In addition, a longer timeframe gives the carriers more time to recover costs and recover from adverse times. For these reasons a longer surrender penalty should enable an annuity to pay a higher rate than one with a shorter penalty. Another advantage of a longer surrender period is it allows the carriers to pay a higher agent commission because the cost has a longer time to be recovered. However, there is no evidence to support the view that the high surrender charges needed to support high commissions is somehow a good thing for the consumer. The bottom line is all costs, whether they are carrier expenses or representatives commissions, reduce the interest paid to the consumer, and higher costs mean less for the annuityowner.

No Surrender

Fixed immediate annuities typically cannot be surrendered. In addition, there are certain "longevity insurance" types of deferred annuity policies that promise to pay a life income beginning at a future date and they may be structured to be unsurrenderable. The advantage is the carrier is able to offer a higher yield due to the certainty of the asset.

MVA

Market Value Adjustments (MVA) were designed by actuaries to make it impossible for representatives to inform annuity buyers of what the actual surrender charges will be. Annuities with MVA are now frequently tied to the DAAJTM (Don't Ask And Just Trust Me) sales approach pioneered in the last century.

Although many representatives I have spoken with tend to believe the previous paragraph, the proclaimed reason behind Market Value Adjustments is the one found in the "Buyer's Guide To Fixed Deferred Annuities" produced by the National Association of Insurance Commissioners which states "Since you and the insurance company share the risk, an annuity with an MVA feature may credit a higher rate than an annuity without that feature". The reasoning is this:

- Insurance companies typically buy bonds to back their annuities.

- Issued bonds decrease in value when market interest rates are rising and increase in value in a falling interest rate environment (if that seems confusing there is a primer on how bonds work at the end of this chapter). If an annuity owner gets out early the carrier needs to recapture the previous costs not yet paid for (commissions, bonuses, administrative costs), and is affected by any changes in value of the assets backing the annuity. If the annuity owner shares in any future declines in asset values the carrier's risk, and money set aside to cover possible asset losses, is reduced and the carrier should pass this savings on to the consumer in the form of a higher return.

That is the theory. Is it reality? I do not know. From a pricing standpoint having MVA does free up money. My problem is it is difficult to make comparisons on the returns of MVA and non-MVA annuities because often one carrier's annuities all use or do not use MVA, and differences in returns between two carriers' annuities may be due to some other factors.

In the last few years MVAs reduced or even eliminated penalties if the annuity was surrendered early because interest rates were falling. In a cycle of rising rates MVA do result in higher than listed surrender costs. However, it is important to remember that Market Value Adjustments do not come into play if the annuity is not surrendered early.

Suitable Liquidity

What is a suitable surrender charge? If the annuityowner will need their entire premium in six months then any surrender charge would be unsuitable. If the annuity is never to be touched because it will be left to heirs then any surrender charge would be suitable. The answer is a suitable surrender charge is one that meets the consumer's liquidity needs in conjunction with other assets owned.

Capital Risk

Several years ago I began researching the question of fixed annuity losses because I had heard unsupported claims for years that annuity owners had either lost principal due to carrier failures, or, conversely, that no annuity owners had ever lost money, and I personally wanted to see if there was any truth out there. I even offered a bounty to anyone that could get me hard information on failed insurers, and out of the nine leads received (and $500 I paid out) I was able to find one carrier that did not return 100 cents on every dollar. Inter-American Companies, an employee benefits carrier with some annuities got into trouble in the '80s and liquidated in 1991; too early to be completely covered by guarantee funds. Out of $648,747 that was still due from the annuities, the owners received a final payout of $97,653.

Four Failed Fixed Annuity Carriers Did Not Return 100 Cents On All Dollars

Since then I have found three more carriers where annuityowners with values over state guaranty fund limits did not receive 100 cents on the dollar. My research discovered owners of annuities issued by London Pacific Life, National American Life Insurance Company of Pennsylvania, and Summit National Life Insurance did receive up to state guaranty limits but account amounts above those limits may never be fully paid. It appears that holders of these annuity contracts received a little over 90 cents on the dollar on account values in excess of state guaranty limits, but that in all cases amounts up to state guaranty fund limits were protected. There may be other carriers out there that have not returned a hundred cents on the annuity dollar, but I sure cannot find them. I can still affirm that no index annuity owner has ever lost a dime due to company failure.

Executive Life
The case most often cited as an example of fixed annuity holders getting back less than their principal is Executive Life. After going through more court briefs and decade-old reports than anyone would want to, I can safely say that people that **surrendered** their annuities when Aurora National Life Assurance Company took over Executive Life's business did take a hit to principal – those opting out of the reorganization process were only promised 56% of their account value, and even annuity owners staying with the new carrier did not receive 100% of their accumulated account value. However, **I can find no evidence** that would support a statement saying **that fixed annuity owners** that stayed the course ultimately **got back less than 100% of their original principal.**

A Comparison Of Bank & Annuity Safety

Over the years I have seen annuity purveyors try to compare the safety of their fixed annuity offering with the bank. I have often heard representatives talk about the "legal reserve system" and say that annuities have much higher reserves backing them than do bank accounts. I have heard representatives tell consumers that, "the bank only has $1.02 behind each savings account dollar while insurance carriers have $1.04 to $1.06 in reserves backing each annuity dollar." However, from my conversations with actuaries and others it appears that this talk results from taking a part of an explanation someone created years ago to try to explain policy surplus and reserves and it has now become a kind of condensed urban legend that many representatives use to try to compare banks and insurance companies. Here is the reality.

Legal Reserves

The states require that an insurance company must keep enough money to cover the current and future obligations of the policies issued, plus a little bit extra. This money is referred to as policy reserves, statutory reserves or legal reserves. The states that the insurance company does business in check out the books of the carrier to ensure there are adequate reserves to cover obligations.

On an individual policy basis what the carrier does is look at the greatest present value of all possible benefit streams, but never less than the cash surrender value of the annuity. On a statutory reserve or legal reserve basis this could translate into insurer reserves equaling anywhere from 100% to 106% or more of cash value.

There is not an insurance company system with special "legal reserve examiners" looking at carrier books. "Legal Reserve" is only an accounting term that means reserves are set aside to cover possible expenses. States audit the insurer's books on a regular basis to make sure sufficient funds are available to cover obligations.

However, the concept of calculated reserves for the bulk of liabilities is possibly unique to the insurance industry. You cannot make an apples-to-apples comparison between insurers and banks because banks view their liabilities on an account value basis and not by reserve valuation.

Capital & Surplus

Because banks do not provide policy benefits another form of comparison would be to look at the capital & surplus of the insurer as a percentage of assets and compare this number with the capital & retained earnings of the bank as a percentage of bank assets.

A while back I looked at the assets and capital surplus for of the twenty largest sellers of index annuities and computed their *Capital Surplus Ratio*. I used the NAIC definition of Capital & Surplus which is "the outstanding capital stock, preferred stock, paid in capital and unassigned funds held for policyholders (assets minus liabilities)" and divided this by the total assets.

The median capital surplus ratio for the twenty largest sellers was 5.9%. Ratios for the twenty carriers ranged from 3.5% to 16.2%.

The capital required for a bank is determined by statute and regulator guidelines. Tier 1 capital is the core measure of a banks financial strength from a regulators point of view; it consists of common stock, irredeemable preferred stock and retained earnings.

The capital ratio is the percentage of a banks capital to its assets and would be a kindred measurement to the capital surplus ratio. To be well-capitalized under federal bank regulatory agency definitions, a bank must have a Tier 1 capital ratio of at least 6%. When I did the research the average capital ratio for all banks was 10.1%.

The largest annuity carriers had average capital ratios of 5.9% vs. 10.1% for the average bank

If you compare these annuity carriers with the average bank the typical annuity carrier has 5.9 cents behind each dollar of assets and the average bank has 10.1 cents behind each dollar of assets. This ratio is on the high side based on bank history. For example, in 2002 there were between 6 and 7 cents backing each bank dollar.

FDIC & Guarantees

A few representatives have told me they explain to their prospects how little money there really is at the FDIC – perhaps believing that bashing a federally insured instrument will make a non-federally insured instrument look safer. Let's look at the realities of FDIC and state insurance guaranty funds.

FDIC is an independent agency of the federal government that was created in 1933 in response to the thousands of bank failures that occurred in the 1920s and early 1930s. Since the start of FDIC insurance in January 1934 no depositor has lost a single cent of insured funds as a result of a bank failure.

State Guaranty Funds were created by state legislatures to protect life, annuity and health insurance policyholders and beneficiaries of an insolvent insurance company. All insurance companies licensed to write life or health insurance or annuities in a state are required, as a condition of doing business in the state, to be members of the guaranty association. If a member company becomes insolvent, money to continue coverage or pay claims is obtained through assessments of other insurance companies writing the same kinds of insurance as the insolvent company.

In 1983 the state guaranty associations founded the National Organization of Life and Health Insurance Guaranty Associations (NOHLGA). If the insolvency affects three or more states NOHLGA coordinates the development of a plan to protect policyholders. NOHLGA states that when annuity carriers have failed *every holder of a covered annuity...has been given the*

*opportunity to have the policy assumed by another healthy carrier
or had the covered portions of their policies fulfilled by their
guaranty association itself,* from http://www.nolhga.com/
insolvencycorner/main.cfm/location/fundamentals

Limits

FDIC covers up to $250,000 in deposits (at least until the end of
2009) for one owner at one insured bank of nonqualified funds and
up to $250,000 in bank IRAs, and there are different categories of
owners that may allow one to increase coverage.

Guaranty Funds do not cover any portion of a policy in which
investment risk is borne by the individual, such as a variable
annuity, and they may or may not cover guaranteed investment
contracts (a/k/a GICs) or unallocated annuity contracts purchased
by entire retirement plans as a funding vehicle for participants.

Every state (plus Puerto Rico) provides $100,000 in withdrawal
and guaranteed cash values for all other annuities (California: 80%
of the present value up to a maximum of $100,000). Twelve states
(and one District) have higher limits:

- $100,000 ($250,000 – IRA) in Virginia

- $130,000 (adjusted for inflation) in Minnesota

- $200,000 in Utah

- $250,000 in Iowa

- $300,000 in Arkansas, DC, North Carolina, Oklahoma, South
  Carolina and Wisconsin

- $500,000 in Connecticut, New York and Washington

Guaranty associations limit protection to residents of their own
state. You are covered if the failed insurer was licensed in your
state of residence. To find out whether a carrier is covered the state
insurance department should be contacted.

Funding

The Deposit Insurance Fund (DIF) assesses banks based on their risk; the riskier the bank the higher the assessment. Assessments range from 0 to 27 basis points

Guaranty Fund assessment levels are set by the individual states. The vast majority of the states may assess the insurer up to 2% of the premiums paid within that state for the guaranty fund. Five states (Alabama, California, Colorado, Florida and Texas) have a maximum annual assessment of 1%, Rhode Island has a maximum assessment of 3% and South Carolina has a maximum assessment of 4%.

Cash On Hand

The FDIC had $52.166 billion on hand at the end of 2007 to cover $4.35 trillion dollars of deposits. Currently the FDIC account represents 1.2% of deposits, but FDIC has the authority to borrow billions of dollars more.

FDIC has $52 billion of cash sitting around in case a bank fails. How much cash do NOHLGA and the collective state guaranty funds have stashed away? The answer is zero, zilch, nada.

In response to my specific question a director of NOHLGA wrote back "It is important to remember that unlike the FDIC, the guaranty system is not pre-funded. Instead, member companies are assessed by the associations only when funds are needed."

Myths & Safety Reality

Legal Reserve is an accounting term and not a special annuity department in the federal government (which is what a representative told me when I explained what legal reserve really meant). The typical bank has a higher percentage of capital backing their depositors than an insurer does backing its policyowners.

In the last quarter century I found 4 failed annuity carrier whereby some policyowners did not get back all of their money (although 3 were covered up to state guarantee fund limits), and even though FDIC cash on hand covers only 1.20% of insured bank deposits, it has $52 billion more than insurer guaranty funds have sitting in their piggybank. I would say that an FDIC insured bank account is safer than a fixed annuity if the entity goes belly up. But the real question is not which is safer, it is "are fixed annuities also safe?"

Every bank customer covered by FDIC and every fixed annuity owner covered by a guaranty fund have been made whole up to the limits of FDIC or the guaranty fund.

If It Fails

When FDIC steps in and takes over a bank you can order the coffin and set the time for the wake because the bank is not coming back to life. It is dead. Let us look at some hard numbers. From 1994 through the first part of 2008 there were 84 bank failures. Although CD deposits within federal deposit insurance limits were protected, the same did not hold true for account balances over the insurance limits. Bank account balances above FDIC limits were treated as creditors of the bank, and these customers stood in line to get paid just like other creditors. Savings customers were at the front of the line, but not every customer was made whole.

During the same period customers of 35 life & health carriers received help from state guarantee funds. When state insurance regulators step in they will often attempt rehabilitation of the insurer and there are many insurers that have entered state receivership, been rehabilitated, and emerged from state care. If rehabilitation did not work every state guaranty fund covered up to $100,000 of cash value in the event of final carrier insolvency.

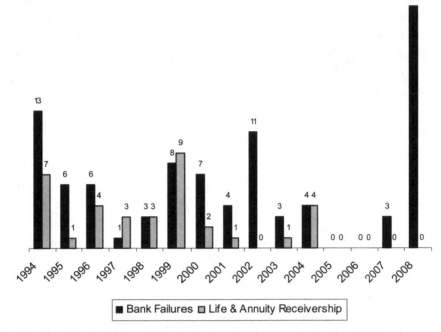

* all CD data is from Federal Reserve Board. Other sources include Federal Deposit Insurance Corp., National Organization of Life and Health Guaranty Associations, National Association of Insurance Commissioners, California, Florida and Illinois Departments of Insurance.

So, Can I Lose Money In A Bank or Fixed Annuity?

Absolutely, if you do not follow the rules you agreed to going in you could lose money. Getting out of a certificate of deposit or fixed annuity early could cause penalties that eat into principal, but if you leave early and incur a loss that was a result of your decision. However, the real question is what is the likelihood of losing your money because the issuer goes under? Even though there have been bank and annuity customers that have lost money due to company failure the reality is this:

Will a consumer lose money due to bank failure with their CD? Almost certainty not.

Will a consumer lose money in their fixed annuity due to an insurer failure? Almost certainly not.

How Strong Is The Carrier?

There are private rating agencies that evaluate the ability of insurers to meet their obligations.

A.M. Best Company (www.ambest.com) is the leading provider of ratings for the insurance industry.

The Fitch Ratings Insurance Group (www.fitchibca.com) provides ratings and research on insurance companies worldwide.

Moody's (www.moodys.com) provides financial strength ratings for life insurance companies.

Standard & Poor's (www.sandp.com) provides ratings and research on insurance companies.

A Primer: Why Bond Values Go Up And Down

Snapshot

When you have stock in a company you are an owner. When you have bonds of a company you are a lender. As a lender you are promised that the company will redeem the bonds at the end of a specified period of time (*the maturity date*) and in the interim the company (*issuer*) will pay you for the use of your money (*interest*). If the company goes bankrupt the lenders (*bondholders*) have dibs on any company assets up to the amount they are owed before the owners (*stockholders*) get paid.

The likelihood of a bond meeting its obligations is often assessed by independent rating agencies. The top four ratings – AAA to BBB if rated by Standard & Poor's, Aaa to Baa if rated by Moody's – are referred to as investment grade. Bonds with ratings below these top four levels are called high yield, non-investment grade, or junk. The lower the rating the higher the interest paid on the bond. The reason why is because lower ratings means higher risk of the bond not meeting obligations and higher risk often translates into a demand for higher returns.

There are many types of bonds. Some bonds are backed by real estate or other physical assets; if the issuer fails to pay (*defaults*) on these bonds the bondholder gets the pledged asset. Many bonds are *debentures* and backed by the full faith and credit of the issuer instead of being secured by a specific asset. There are also *convertible bonds* wherein the bondholder has the right to exchange the bond for a specified number of shares of stock.

More Terms

Bonds are generally issued in denominations of $1000 (*par value*), but quoted as parts of a hundred. The newspaper may report that a particular bond sold at 92. What this means is the bond sold for 92% of $1000 or $920. A bond sold for less than $1000 is said to be selling at a *discount*. A bond selling for more than $1000 is selling at a *premium*. Whether sold at a discount or a premium the company will pay $1000 (the par value) at maturity. Some bonds may be redeemed by the issuer prior to maturity; these are *callable bonds*.

A bond has a *coupon rate*. This is the rate of interest that is paid out on the $1000 bond, usually on a semiannual basis. A coupon rate of 6% means the issuer would cut a check for $30 twice a year. There are also *zero-coupon bonds* that do not pay regular interest and sell at a discount, with the par value paid at maturity. A commonly owned zero-coupon bond is a Series EE Saving Bond. The coupon rate is affected by the time until maturity – usually the longer the wait until the bond matures the higher the rate, special provisions – callable bonds typically have higher coupon rates and convertible bonds have lower coupon rates, and the financial strength of the issuer – stronger companies pay lower rates than financially weaker companies.

Yields

The *current yield* is the coupon rate paid divided by the price of the bond. If the coupon rate is 6% the bond is producing $60 of interest a year. If the bond cost $1000 the current yield would also be 6% ($60/$1000 = .06 or 6%). If the bond cost $800 the current yield would be 7.5% ($60/$800 = 7.5%). If the bond cost $1200 the current yield would be 5% ($60/$1200 = 5%)

The *yield to maturity* reflects the coupon rate, the premium or discount when the bond was purchased, and the number of years until the bond matures. Let us say the bond matures in ten years. If you paid $1000 for the bond, and receive $60 in interest income, your yield to maturity is 6%, which is the same as your coupon rate.

But what if you paid $800 for this bond? Not only are you getting $60 in annual interest, but in ten years you will make an additional $200 when you redeem that $1000 bond that you bought for $800. Or what if you paid $1200 for the bond? You may be getting $60 each year, but you are going to take a $200 loss when you get back the par value of $1000 a decade hence for the $1200 you spent today.

Yield to maturity takes into account any difference between price paid and redemption price, and reflects the time value of any discount or premium. Yield to maturity is not calculated by simply dividing any premium or discount by the years until maturity, adding or subtracting this amount from the coupon interest, and then dividing the result by $1000, because that ignores the time value of money.

Using the previous example, the actual yield to maturity for the bond with a 6% coupon and ten years until maturity that was purchased for $800 is 9.09%. If the same bond was purchased for $1200 the yield to maturity is 3.60%. You need to use bond tables or a good financial calculator to determine the real yield to maturity.

Coupon Rate	Current Yield	Yield to Maturity	Bond Price
6%	6.00%	6.00%	$1000
6%	7.50%	9.09%	$ 800
6%	5.00%	3.60%	$1200

Why Bond Prices Drop When Rates Go Up

When interest rates go up existing bonds lose value, because new bonds are more attractive. In our example the bond has a 6% coupon rate and pays $60 a year interest. If bonds with similar maturity dates and creditworthiness also had 6% coupon rates our bond would sell for $1000.

But what if new 1-year bonds were paying 7% coupon rates? No one is going to give us $1000 for a bond paying $60 when they can get $70 on a new one. They would give us less than $1000 for our bond. How much less?

To produce a current yield of 7% with coupon interest of $60 means our bond would be worth $857.14. However, bond prices are based on the yield to maturity reflecting any discounts or premiums on par value. To earn a 7% yield to maturity on a 6% coupon with a ten year maturity requires a price of $928.94.

And The Reverse Is Also True

What if new ten-year bonds were paying 5% interest and our bond has a coupon rate of 6%. Based on a 5% yield to maturity, our bond would be worth $1077.94. Of course, if you simply held on to the bond you would get $1000 back at maturity.

The following chart reflects the effect of interest rate changes on a bond with a 6% coupon rate and ten year maturity.

Coupon Rate	Yield to Maturity	Bond Price	Gain (Loss)
6%	4.00%	$1163	16.3%
6%	5.00%	$1078	7.8%
6%	6.00%	$1000	-0-
6%	7.00%	$ 929	(7.1%)
6%	8.00%	$ 864	(13.6%)
6%	9.00%	$ 805	(19.5%)

Other Factors

Since the coupon rate of most bonds usually remains unchanged and does not rise if the cost of living increases, bond prices are also affected by inflation. Long maturities subject bonds to greater inflation risk and typically require high yields to compensate.

Another major element in the price of a bond is the financial strength of the issuer. Bond buyers demand higher yields as concerns about the ability of the issuer to meet obligations increase. Higher risk demands higher yield. If a rating agency cuts a bond's credit rating a higher yield is needed, reducing the value of the bond, and reflecting the perceived increase in risk.

Sales Points

➤ Every fixed annuity owner covered by a guaranty fund has been made whole up to the limits of the guaranty fund

Chapter 4 – Financial Myths & Illusions

Consumers make normal decisions. Normal decisions contain rational pieces, behavioral elements and illusions that all combine in the decision-making process and result in the final decision. This chapter deals with beliefs that consumers think are factual when they are often illusions or financial myths.

These myths and illusions often get in the way of a sale and by showing the consumer that their belief is an illusion a possible objection is overcome. Financial illusions do not always work against the sale, sometimes they can work in favor of the annuity

General Illusions

Projection Bias

We use it in predicting tomorrow's weather. We use it in sports to predict winning or losing streaks. And we certainly use it with money. It is called *projection bias* and what it means is taking what happened yesterday and today and thinking it is going to happen tomorrow. The problem is that is often wrong.

Stock Market Index

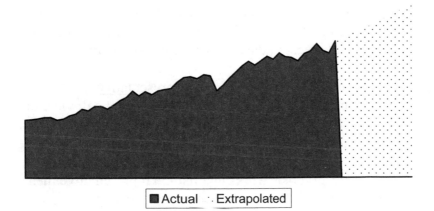

■ Actual ·· Extrapolated

As an example, the green part of this chart shows actual steadily rising index movement for a three year period. If you were to ask people where the index would go for the next three years most of them would continue seeing an upward slope into the future.

However, this period was from 1996 to 1999 and we all know what really happened to the stock market over the next three years.

S&P 500 March 96 - March 02

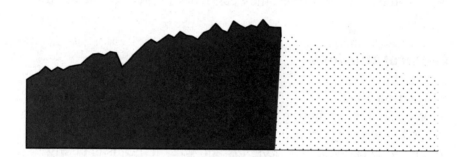

Projection bias causes us to take what we think we are seeing from existing data and then extrapolating the known data into an unknown tomorrow. Although estimating future values from existing data may work in algebra class it doe not work well in the financial world because the future value of the stock market and interest rates are not mathematical certainties, but instead depend on how real people react to the changing financial world.

What does projection bias mean for the representative?
If the consumer's projection bias creates a crystal ball view of the future that supports the representative, then nothing needs to be said – the consumer may be making the right choice for the wrong reason but they are making the right choice. However, if the consumer's projection bias works against the representative then the consumer's view of the future path needs to change.

72

CD Rates

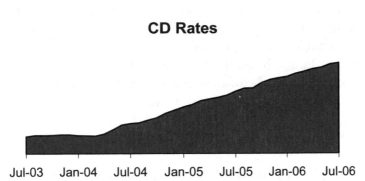

Jul-03 Jan-04 Jul-04 Jan-05 Jul-05 Jan-06 Jul-06

This chart explains why fixed annuity sales fell in 2006. CD rates rose dramatically in 2004, 2005, and 2006. If you extend the blue line you could probably guess where consumers were predicting CD rates would be in 2007. Consumers were thinking why should they lock into an annuity when CD rates would keep going up?

The reality is CD rates flattened and then began to fall, which is why fixed annuity sales picked up. However, if the representative did not want to sit out 2007 and wait until reality caught up with projections, then the consumer's view needed to be changed.

CD Rates

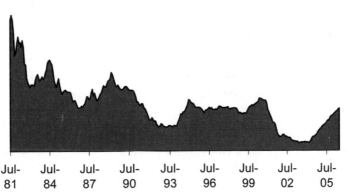

Jul-81   Jul-84   Jul-87   Jul-90   Jul-93   Jul-96   Jul-99   Jul-02   Jul-05

One can counter a projection bias that interferes with the annuity purchase. For example, if a consumer is projecting steadily- rising rates a chart showing how rates have actually declined over the last 25 years may bring needed perspective and help a consumer understand that a "rate in the hand" protects them against uncertainty. Magnified consumer concerns created by extrapolating today's headlines into future stock market moves may be countered by "zooming out" and using a chart of longer term stock market movements that show the direct opposite of these concerns.

If The Past Works Against You Change The Past

Consumers often are operating from a perspective of projection bias and this bias sometimes gets in the way of their buying an annuity. The way to counter this bias is to show the consumer an alternative projection. This is not about manipulating the future – the future is unknown and cannot be manipulated. It is simply showing that taking yesterday and today and saying the same pattern will continue tomorrow is an illusion. One needs to understand what the bias is so that it can be addressed.

Projection Bias: What Can Be Done
Have three charts available showing a period when the stock market was rising, the stock market was falling, and one where certificate of deposit rates are falling.

Vividness Bias

If a representative is offering an annuity paying 5% interest while a competitor's annuity is paying 6%, the representative could mention that the competitor is paying 1% more interest. However, if a representative is offering an annuity paying 5% interest while a competitor's annuity is paying 4%, the representative should shout, "I CAN GET YOU 25% MORE INTEREST!"

The idea behind *vividness bias* is people react strongly to louder, brighter, and bigger. Vividness can be used to emphasize strengths and play down weakness. What it means is making the positives of what is being offered sound as big as possible and making any negatives sound as small as possible.

<table>
<tr><td>I can get you 10% more.</td><td><h2>I CAN GET YOU
$10,000 MORE!</h2></td></tr>
</table>

To illustrate, suppose a consumer has $100,000 available to buy a fixed annuity and the annuity has a 10% premium bonus. The premium bonus could be described as a 10% enhancement to the annuity, or the representative could say, "I can get you TEN THOUSAND DOLLARS." Which appeal sounds bigger?

Now, if that same annuity also had a surrender penalty of 10% the representative probably would not want to say, "You know if you get out of this big boy in six months you are going to pay a $10,000 penalty." Instead, the penalty should be referred to as a 10% penalty, or perhaps one could say the penalty is a tenth of the premium. If you remember back to third grade math, there is a biological reason for why fractions were so difficult. People do not process fractions well and when we hear financial concepts expressed in fractions it often does not get through – people do not always hear the fraction.

This bias often overwhelms the rational mind. A college study asked people which disease was more dangerous, Disease A that killed 1,286 people out of every 10,000 or Disease B that killed 24% of the population. The majority of the folks said A was deadlier, even though A's real mortality was roughly half of B (12.86%). The reason is 1,286 is bigger than 24%.

One way to show vividness is to make a greater contrast. Putting 17 ounces of ice cream in a quart container is about half-full; 17 ounces in a pint container is over the top. Which looks like more?

Which contrast makes the annuity return seem more vivid? Showing a stack of 40 dimes to illustrate the 4% annuity interest earned versus a stack of 30 dimes showing the bank interest paid on $100, or putting down 4 dollar bills and 3 dollar bills?

6% Yield	7% Yield

In an annuity context using vividness bias might mean presenting sales materials with the promoted annuity interest rate in bold yellow letters on a red background, while showing competitor's rates in dark gray type on a light gray page. Vividness is hard to fight against, which is why marketers often rely on it to raise interest in what they are selling.

A place where vividness bias really goes in two directions is where there is the possibility of a very positive or very negative event each with a low probability of occurring. It does not matter if the probability is 1 in a thousand or 1 in a million if the probability is based on the possibility of winning the lottery or having cancer, because we tend to take extreme events and give them only two magnitudes – probably will not happen or probably will happen – and ignore the real odds. We also give extreme events a higher likelihood of occurring than they deserve – the odds of dying in a terrorist attack are infinitesimally smaller than dying in a house fire caused by lightning, but we require everyone to take their shoes off at the airport but not to install lightning rods on their homes.

Extreme event vividness bias could cause a consumer to drastically overestimate the possibility of losing money if their fixed annuity carrier failed. Telling the consumer that in the last two decades annuityowners in only 3 carriers failed to receive all of their money because the insurer failed (discussed in the Safety Chapter) may not soothe them because what they are hearing is that 100% of the 3 failed carriers failed. It may be better to show the failure rate related to how many annuity carriers did not fail.

The Black Portion Shows % of Failed Annuity Carriers

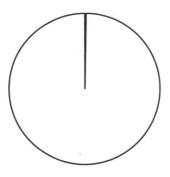

The vividness of a product's benefits may be more important than the benefits themselves. Even if ten products offer the same benefits, the one with the most vivid message stands the best odds of being purchased.

Vividness Bias: What Can Be Done
Describe the positive aspects in ways that make then seem larger and mention negative points in ways that make them look smaller. Although this can be done by using larger type sizes or brighter colors it can also be done by using the math term that contains the most zeros when your message is positive ($10,000 not 10%) and the fewest zeros when communicating a negative point (1/10 not $10,000).

Another way to use Vividness Bias is to create anecdotes or pictures. Many of us remember "red sky in morning, sailor take warning." How about creating new sayings such as "annuities are safe, stocks cause waste" or "annuities are strong, banks are wrong." These are silly, but they stick in the mind and may be recalled the next time a decision needs to be made. Or tell the story of how grandpa and grandma were able to keep their yellow polka dot painted house (vivid) because they bought an annuity.

Point Blindness – The Lack of Vividness

The annuity yielded 1%. Is that good? It depends on what it is compared to. As a stand alone point it is a low number, but if the rest of the sentence is ...and if you had left the money in that mutual fund you were in you would have lost 25%"... then that 1% looks pretty good. If your point (number) is perceived as bad or a competitor's point is perceived as better, try to do a comparison that blunts the point.

Risk & Volatility

This wheel has 5 possible outcomes with four of them returning 6% and one returning 1%.

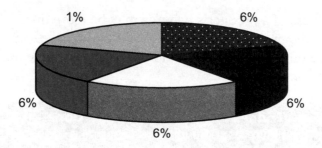

This wheel also has 5 possible outcomes, but they range from 2% to 12%.

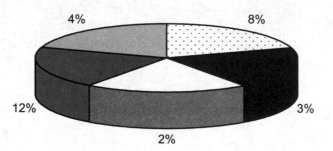

If you spin both wheels, which one is riskier?

If you ask people which wheel has the greatest risk most people say it is the bottom one. And they are right if you only spin the wheels once.

On one spin of the wheel the top wheel has a 20% chance of returning less than 6% and the bottom wheel has a 60% chance of returning less than 6%. On one spin of the wheel the bottom wheel poses the greatest risk of low returns.

However, a consumer's financial world does not consist of one spin of the wheel. A consumer is not taking all of their retirement money and betting it all on how the market does tomorrow. In reality our financial world is made up of thousands of spins of the wheel.

Not Understanding Risk & Volatility
If you spin our two wheels many times the bottom one produces the higher return and is therefore less risky than the top one. Unfortunately, we tend to assume the bottom wheel is riskier because it is more volatile, and because we see the future as one spin of the wheel at a time we confuse volatility and risk. Not understanding the difference between risk and volatility often sabotages plans by causing us to not maximize potential earnings.

Assuming Safety Means Higher Returns
Hand in hand with this is a belief that less principal risky investments have higher returns. I have read several surveys asking retirees whether stocks or bonds produce higher returns over time and the majority choose bonds. Why? Because they believe bonds simply have to produce higher returns since they do not go up and down as much as stocks.

Illusion May Help An Annuity Sale
Risk and volatility are two separate things, and there actually is a relationship between risk and return – taking higher investment risk does usually result in higher returns. But it doesn't seem

correct to most consumers that a vehicle that protects them from market loss should produce a lower return than one that does not.

However, the volatility illusion believed by consumers helps to put money into banks and annuities. Consumers are predisposed to assume that accounts wherein principal is protected and where they believe the earnings have less fluctuation will produce higher returns over time than ones that do not.

What does this mean to the annuity representative? If the representative is presenting a multi-year rate fixed annuity the consumer is seeing that as the "top wheel" and will be inclined to view it favorably.

Or Hurt It

If the representative is presenting an indexed rate annuity and trying to move money from the bank, the consumer is often seeing the index annuity as the "bottom wheel" because of the possibility of years with low or zero indexed benefited interest.

> ### Risk & Volatility: What Can Be Done
> The consumer already tends to see fixed rate annuities as producing competitive returns because the returns are less volatile. The problem may arise when the consumer is nervous about moving money from the bank to an index annuity because of the potential years of zero index-linked interest. The representative should ask whether the consumer will be taking all of the money out of the bank in one year and spending it. If the answer is no, the consumer should be reminded that the annuity may well be less risky over time because it could produce a higher return than if the money stayed in the bank.

Illusions surrounding Risk & Volatility can work for or against the annuity purchase. Wall Street often seems to be a place of continuous illusions. Let us examine some of the more popular ones.

Wall Street Illusions

Wall Street's Retirement Income Plan

An oft proposed Wall Street retirement income plan (Wall Street R.I.P) uses two rules of thumb. The first rule is an age-based asset allocation formula that says *100 minus your age* should equal the percentage of stocks in your portfolio. So, a 60 year old would have 40% stocks and 60% bonds/cash and a 30 year old would have 70% stocks and 30% bonds/cash. The idea behind this is that stocks are more volatile than bonds and have greater risk of loss over the short term; therefore as you get older you should shift more money into less volatile bonds. The second rule of thumb is using a *safe withdrawal rate*. In the '80s and '90s it was commonly said that one could withdraw 5% from their portfolio forever, increased for inflation, and never run out of money. These two rules were used by many retirement planners to advise folks how to allocate and receive their retirement funds.

Using 100-Age your retirement money ran out 1 in 4 times

A few years ago a trio of planners tested these rules. They took actual past market performance and then mixed up the yearly returns to randomly create thousands of different possible financial patterns to show how different mixes of stocks, bonds, and cash would perform if the past parameters repeated. Instead of using a 5% safe withdrawal rate they were even more conservative and used 4.5%, adjusted for inflation.

What they found was if you put 40% into stocks and the rest into bonds and stocks you ran out of money 24% of the time after 30 years and 41% of the time after 35 years. What that means is if a 60 year old followed the 100 - age = % of stocks rule of thumb they would have run out of money by age 90 a quarter of the time and by age 95 two fifths of the time. Even after using a more conservative 4.5% safe withdrawal rate there was a one in four chance the retiree patient would die on the table.

This study was published in 2001. You would think that after seeing the results of a study where one out of four people died that Wall Street and the media would have told everyone "don't use the 100 minus your age thingy with a safe withdrawal rate, we were wrong, it doesn't work very well" but they have not. Instead, the new story is keep using 100 – Age = Stocks but withdraw 4% a year instead of 4.5%. Instead of choosing to correct the allocation illusion, Wall Street and the media instead chose to make it a little less wrong. Some have gone as far as suggesting you should only withdraw 3% from your retirement assets to lower the risk of outliving your money (and if you withdrew nothing I am sure your money would last even longer). But the problem was not solved because the problem is the two rules of thumb do not work well.

Wall Street's R.I.P – the retiree wants so the children can waste

The problem with using these two rules is two things can happen. The first is even at a lower "safe rate" you can still run out of money before you die – taking out 4% or even 3% does not eliminate the risk of running out of money it simply reduces it. The bigger problem, and what is much more likely to happen, is the retiree will live their retirement in penury only to leave their beneficiaries with a mountain of cash – the retiree will want so the children can waste.

I am not the only one that thinks this way. William Sharpe, a developer of the Capital Asset Pricing Model and the Sharpe Ratio for risk analysis, a man that had a huge role in making possible our modern financial tools, said about the two retirement rules of thumb that "Either the spending or the investment rule can be a part of an efficient strategy, but together they create either large surpluses or result in a failed spending plan." The bottom line is Wall Street's long suggested retirement income plan does not work well.

> Wall Street and the financial media have so much invested in preserving these twin retirement planning illusions that it can be difficult for the representative to overcome the bias. Frankly, I would get a copy of the 2001 study, show it to consumers, and ask if they want to play the Wall Street R.I.P. lottery.

Historical Returns & Other Delusions

A lack of future knowledge is why all planning for tomorrow is always a matter of guessing, gambling and superstition, even though it is disguised as science by the use of computer models and financial formulas. Millions of people construct retirement plans purporting to say what a mix of assets will return over the next ten, twenty or forty years, and if this arrogant presumption of prophecy is not bodacious enough many people attach labels setting forth "confidence levels" of the data produced. The problem with all of this forecasting is it always attempts to extrapolate the past into the future and except in the broadest terms the financial past does not repeat.

<u>Boom and Bust</u>

I can prove that the average market return for the 1990s should have been 9.8%. It's simply a matter of looking at the stock market returns of the previous century, calculating averages and standard deviations, doing a few dozen linear regressions, and ta-da! In fact John Bogle, founder of Vanguard, wrote an article as the decade began saying, "during the 1990s stocks will have their work cut out for themselves to exceed returns in the 8% to 12% range." Based on my models I can state with 98% certainty there is no way the 1990s could produce an annualized return of over 14%! However, the real stock market return for the previous decade was not 9.8% it was 17.8%.

That was on the boom side. On the bust side I can show with better than 90% probability that the market will not go down three years in a row. A bear market, yes, but ending after a one or two year decline. However, the millennium bear market resulted in index declines ranging from 35% to 75% and losses for calendar years 2000, 2001 and 2002. Oops.

Now, if you take a broader look and extend the '90s through 2003 – create a 13 year decade – you get an annualized return of between 10% and 11%. Does this mean my original 10% projection was pretty much correct but it simply took a little longer to happen, or was I dead wrong, but by making enough adjustments I can make any numbers fit my preconceived conclusion?

Retirement planning formulas provide an accurate forecast providing nothing unforeseen happens, the world does not change, and tax laws and investment strategies are not adjusted based on emotions and fads.

Unfortunately, I believe it is the latter (which is why economics is called the dismal science). I'm not alone in my concern over how the past is misused. Even William Sharpe, a Nobel Prize winning economist mentioned earlier said, "Past average experience may be a terrible predictor of future performance."

What I think all this means is not to take too seriously financial plans that show you will need an income of $82,000 in 2035 based on a 5.4% "safe rate" and assuming a 3.2% inflation rate requiring $1,518,519 of principal thus necessitating an annual investment of $16,075 that will naturally earn a 7% average yield all with a 97% confidence level, providing nothing unforeseen happens, the world does not change, and tax laws and investment strategies are not adjusted based on emotions and fads.

Driving Via The Rear View Mirror
Although the inflation-adjusted annual returns of stocks has been around 6% for long periods within the last two centuries the same cannot be said for bonds. The inflation-adjusted return on government bonds was 5.1% from 1802 to 1870 but averaged 0.5% annually when calculated over most of the 20th century. A key

problem with the Wall Street models is they all assume the next century will perform like the last, or to be more specific, the next 30 years will be within the parameters of market moves over the last 80 years. I believe that this is a questionable assumption.

The following chart shows the simple average annual "after-inflation" gain or loss of the stock market average for 600 thirty year periods beginning in 1928. What I did was calculate the annual gain or loss for each year of the subsequent 30 year period, subtract the rate of inflation for the period, add the inflation-adjusted 30 numbers together, divide by 30 and get an average simple annual gain or loss (movement for 9/28 to 9/29 + 9/29 to 9/30 +....9/57 to 9/58: all divided by 30) and then did it again and again (10/28 to 10/29 + 10/29 to 10/30 +....10/57 to 10/58: all divided by 30). The idea was to see what the average market inflation-adjusted annual gain or loss would have been for, say, the 30 years following a retirement in October 1928, November 1928, all the way up to retiring in October 1978.

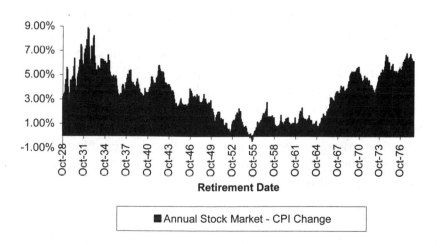

Avg Inflation Adjusted Annual Gain/Loss For Following 30 Yr Period If Bottom Axis Is 1st Day Of Retirement

What I found was there were extreme differences between

85

periods. If you had retired in June 1932 the average net gain was 8.75% a year for the next 30 years, but if you retired in June 1955 the net showed an annual simple loss after inflation when calculated annually until June 1985. In general if you retired in the 1950s or early 1960s the average net gain over the next 30 years was very low – 0% to 2%, primarily due to the lousy '70s stock market and the inflation of the '70s and early '80s.

It is important to note that these numbers do not include reinvested dividends. Dividends would have added 2%, 4% or even more to the average annual change, depending on the period. It should also be noted that these are simple and not compound results. Gains are not added back in and losses are not deducted. You cannot use this chart to say, "you would have earned an x% return if you had bought the stocks in October 1946."

The point of this chart is to show that even tho the long-term stock market return has been around 6% after inflation for the last 200 years you cannot rely on that number for planning a 30 year retirement. Even if past performance predicts the future – something every prospectus says does not happen – a retiree cannot be sure which past will repeat.

The bigger problem is even though the required mantra is that the past does not predict the future most of these Wall Street models depend on the past repeating in some fashion, because if the past truly does not predict the future – as they are all required to say – their models are essentially useless. The financial climate has changed, financial tools have changed, and global demographics have changed. It may be true that beyond recognizing there are economic cycles, that the accuracy of all Wall Street retirement models are no better than throwing darts at a retirement allocation dartboard.

What I believe is you need to remember long, long-term financial trends while taking into account short-term realities. For example, a tax-deferred dollar of interest should be worth more instead of current taxes for those future need dollars. But, if you believe your tax rate might be higher when you withdraw your tax-deferred dollars than when you put them in, adjust your plan and do not defer your taxes.

The stock market has produced risk-adjusted returns higher than those of bonds, but periods of less than five years, and even ten years, can be problematic if you are withdrawing income from stocks. So, perhaps you could invest most of the long-term money in the stock market, but when you get within ten years of spending the money take another look at short-term realities and make necessary adjustments.

And maybe if your plan requires a 5% annual yield for income, but returns are down and you only make 4% one year, it might be better to simply tighten your belt and spend a little less rather than increasing the risk aspect of your portfolio and disrupting your plans to get that higher return. Do not get hung on prophesized numbers, learn and apply long-term concepts, and adjust as needed.

When 10% Minus 6% Equals Zero

It can be argued that the stock market has averaged a 10% non-inflation-adjusted annual return over the last 80 year or so. If that 10% average holds true in the future one might assume that taking out 6% a year would give you plenty of buffer for down times and your money would last forever. After all, earning 10% and spending 6% means you are leaving 4% to grow and compound. Unfortunately, averaging 10% does not mean earning 10% each year and therein lays the problem.

If you have a ten year period that looks like the following chart the annualized average return is 10%. If you put $100,000 in, and left it alone, ten years later you'd have $260,000. However, if you began withdrawing $6,000 a year in the first year – a 6% spending rate – you run out of money. The obvious reason is the combination of withdrawals and dramatic market drops in years one and two put you so far down that you never recover.

Starting with $100,000 & Withdrawing $6000/Yr

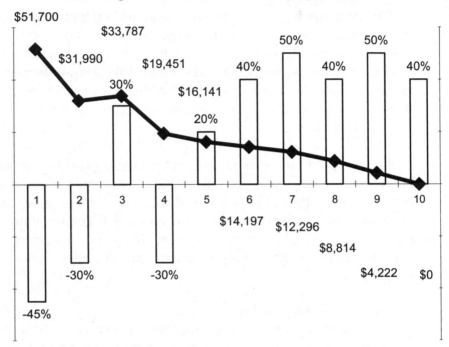

If you look at the 25 years from 1981 to 2006 the S&P 500 Index averaged 10% a year and not only could you have maintained your 6% income but you would have a ended up with an end balance of roughly $4 for every $1 you started with. However, if you look at the 25 years from 1973 to 1998 the S&P 500 also averaged 10% a year, but you ran out of money in 1992. If you play with more periods you find that you were okay if you started withdrawals in 1970 or 1971, but if you began withdrawals in 1968 or 1969 you also ran out of money before the 25 years were up.

Wall Street Illusions: Avoiding The Full Market Monte

The uncertainty of future income is the problem with Wall Street's R.I.P. To avoid running out of money you may be forced to make retirement into a bitter, penny-pinching experience that leaves buckets of money for your heirs, or because of market risk you might spend too much and wind up needing to live with those heirs.

One obvious solution is to buy a life-only immediate annuity. If you do not have a bequest need then the logical answer is to maximize your income and eliminate the potential of losing it. Indeed, the last time I checked an age 66 man could get a 6% income for life, indexed for inflation, and never outlive his money. You could provide a couple an income for as long as either lived. The problem is most people do not seem to be able to cope with the psychological problem of losing the asset when it is converted into an immediate annuity.

Another problem with these retirement probabilities is assuming people will act like computers when a future crisis occurs. However, people act normally and thus react emotionally to events, which mean computer-like decisions may not be made in times of stress. Instead of building your retirement life around a 4% withdrawal retirement plan that ignores the twin realities that the future is unknown and retirees are not computers, I believe it makes more sense to develop contingency plans to give you a guide to follow if certain things do happen.

Try Not To Retire In A Down Period

It is New Years Day 2001, the year you planned to retire, but the market has dropped over 10% in the last six months. Perhaps you should delay retirement and wait and see. Using the S&P 500 as a proxy for the market, if we had $100,000 and took out an inflation-adjusted $4,000 a year beginning in 2001 we only had $74,108 left by the end of 2006 (and it got down to $60,000 before the 2003 bull market kicked in). But if we had delayed retirement for two years we would be sitting with $138,000 today.

If you recently retired perhaps you should consider doing some part-time work that will help keep your hands out of the retirement cookie jar until the market turns.

Try To Spend Less In A Down Period

The retirement math models all assume that withdrawal amounts increase each year, but that may not reflect reality. I have listened to hundreds of retirees over the past score of years and in general I have found they try to match their outgo to their income. If the retirees' bank CD is paying 5% this year instead of 4% they spend the extra 1%. If the mutual fund dividend gets cut from $600 to $400 a year then $200 less is spent at home. If the income reflects what is happening to the principal I have seen retirees adjust to the income, and a few years of taking a little less may put a detoured retirement engine back on track (using the previous example if you had retired in 2001 and spent 3% in 2002 and 2003 instead of 4% you would have had $80,000 by 2006 instead of $74,000).

Is everyone able to postpone retirement, work at a part-time job, or tighten their belt to get thru market downturns? Of course not, but many retirees can react to these challenges, and by reacting as people instead of computer models the retirees can help maintain their retirement funds.

Put 10% to 15% In A Safe Place

Beginning with $100,000 at the end of 1972, if you withdrew an inflation-adjusted $4500 from the S&P 500 starting in 1973 you ran out of money in 1993. However, if you could have put $90,000 in the S&P 500, placed the remaining $10,000 in a no-market-risk vehicle to produce the $4,500 withdrawals until it was used up, and then started taking inflation-adjusted $4,500 withdrawals from what was left of the original $90,000 in the S&P 500, you did not run out of money in 1993.

It appears putting 10% to 15% of the retirement money into no-market-risk vehicles and withdrawing this money during market downturns instead of tapping into the invested assets may help money survive longer.

Magical GLWB

The Guaranteed Lifetime Withdrawal Benefit available on many annuities gives income for life and control of the asset. The main disadvantage is the payout is not indexed to inflation. However, most annuity GLWBs have reset or step-up provisions that allow for increased income if the benefit base increases. In addition, while most financial plans would suggest a 4% withdrawal starting point for a 70 year old the typical fixed annuity GLWB would pay out 6% or more. At 3% inflation the retiree would be age 85 before the financial plan income exceeded the GLWB income (and that assumes no increases in the GLWB benefit base and all of the excess GLWB income is spent on enjoying retirement and not reinvested).

And You Can Always Buy An Income Annuity

Using our 2001 retirement example we would have had $74,000 remaining at the end of 2006. Adjusted for inflation we would now be withdrawing $4,776 a year or an equivalent of 6.45% of the remaining principal.

If we no longer want to perform a full market monte and be totally exposed to market risk, we could buy an inflation-adjusting life payout immediate annuity. The last time I checked $74,000 would produce $5,000 annually that increases as inflation increases.

Dark Illusions – Bogus Names & Inexperts

The previous examples of financial illusions are things that people do to themselves because of our prehistoric past. We take what happened yesterday and today and project it into tomorrow because that shows us the migration path of the mastodon that we hunt, and the vividness of the danger of the saber tooth tiger helps to protect us to live another day. The problem is humans have never fully adapted to the modern world and so we react to these impulses born in a distant past and try to use them in the financial world. However, there are other financial illusions that are created specifically to manipulate consumers.

A Rose By Any Other Name Still Smells

Want a surefire method to increase investment sales? Change your product's name to reflect today's hot financial trend and advertise heavily. Are hedge funds creating sales? Great, change the name of your investment to "The Investment Hedge." Is gold getting a lot of airplay? Fine, call your product the "Gold Fund."

What if your investment does not act like a hedge fund or does not own any gold? It does not matter; sales will increase anyway, even if your yields are below average, because folks will buy as long as the name is right.

63% of Mutual Fund name changes were done simply to mislead investors

A trio of academics examined whether mutual funds sometimes change their names to take advantage of trendy investment styles, but do not change the way they invest to match their new name. Their finding was that 63% of the 296 mutual fund name changes that occurred between 1994 and 2001were purely cosmetic. However, even though the name change was bogus, inflows to these "cosmetic" funds increased just like funds that had actually changed their way of investing (heavy advertising of the trendy new names brought in even more money for both real and cosmetic funds).

The authors state "The implication for fund managers desiring to increase flows is unambiguous: Make a hot style name change, do not worry about your fund's performance...and advertise your fund."

Professional Coin Flipping

Many investors rely on financial professionals to help them in selecting winning equity investments, even though study after study has shown that the average return of the overall stock market has consistently outperformed professional predictions over the long term. Even so, surely the predictive power of these knowledgeable stock analysts and investment professionals is better than the stock predictions made by purely amateur investors? Or perhaps not.

A recent study compared the stock picks of investment professionals (portfolio managers, stockbrokers, analysts) with inexperienced laypeople. The professionals reported their strategy was primarily based on their intricate knowledge of the stock market; the amateurs said they guessed. Both amateurs and professionals believed the financial professionals would do a better job of picking winning stocks.

The outcome? The amateurs picked many more winners than the professionals. In fact, the professionals were only right 40% of the time meaning the professionals would have done significantly better if they'd simply flipped a coin. One should keep in mind that this was a limited study in both time and scope.

Dark Illusions

If someone names their mutual fund the "XYZ High Tech Fund" we trust them to only buy high tech stocks. However, what this shows is that this trust can be misused and the consumer will probably not even know he or she's been had as long as the name was "right."

Consumers assume financial professionals will make better decisions than they themselves would, although in the study this was not the case. The broader implication of the study is not the stock picking ability of professionals, but the trust consumers give to people that say they are professionals. When a consumer meets with a stockbroker, financial services professional or insurance representative they trust that professional to have the answers that will help them, generally without asking for proof to justify that trust.

Annuity Myths From Wall Street

<u>An Annuity Is Just An Income Stream</u>
A fixed annuity is a savings vehicle that offers minimum guarantees, tax advantages <u>and</u> the ability to receive an income one cannot outlive. A study conducted a few year ago found that more than 99% of the fixed annuities purchased are not annuitized, but instead used as a conservative savings instrument offering availability of interest and the ability to pass along assets to a designated beneficiary. And yet the financial media's message is a fixed annuity is an income vehicle, and they tell consumers not to buy one unless they 1) need immediate income and 2) want to lose their principal forever.

The income benefits of a fixed annuity are wonderful. Although you always had the ability to convert a deferred annuity balance into a guaranteed income thru annuitization, the advances in guaranteed lifetime withdrawal benefits give the consumer not only income they cannot outlive but freedom to use the actual annuity account value. Annuity incomes benefits will become even more important in years to come. But the income feature is only one benefit of owning an annuity. Tell the consumer a fixed deferred annuity is:

• A savings vehicle that guarantees you will earn at least a minimum return regardless of where future interest rates go – only

94

Savings Bonds also offer this feature (and you need to wait 20 years to receive it with an EE bond).

- A savings vehicle that gives you a choice of receiving a stated rate of interest or the potential for more interest by receiving stated participation in an external index.

A Fixed Annuity Is A Variable Annuity

Often the financial press will write about annuities, but often the article is about variable annuities. Variable annuities are as far away from fixed annuities as mutual funds are from certificates of deposit, and yet many consumers, and reporters, confuse the two.

When I get a call from a reporter wanting to talk about fixed annuities I always ask them a question – "Do fixed annuities have fees?" If they answer yes, I tell them to go to my web site www.indexannuity.org, and read the article *A Reporter's Guide To Fixed Annuities*. Representatives need to ask consumers the same question and then educate them on what a fixed annuity truly is.

A Fixed Annuity Is Not For Young People

The "too young" slap against annuities is usually based on the IRS rule requiring a 10% penalty on most annuity withdrawals when under age 59½. Whether this really is a factor depends on the comparative returns of other vehicles and what the money is intended to do. If the choice is between a certificate of deposit yielding 2% or a fixed annuity crediting 4%, the annuity still pays more even if hit with the IRS penalty. And if the money is earmarked for retirement saying you should not buy an annuity at age 35 is as nonsensical as saying not to fund an IRA at age 35.

A Fixed Annuity Is Not For Old People

The "too old" criticism usually is based on either misunderstanding what an annuity maturity date is or the surrender charge. Someone will say "an 80 year old should not buy this annuity because they are locked in until age 105." The maturity date referred to is the latest the annuityowner can force the insurer to keep the money and not the other way around. I have found simply stating this is sufficient.

A Maturity Date Is Not Life Without Parole
One of the stranger conclusions I once read was that annuities lock up your money for 40 or 50 years, and the reason is the writer confused maturity date with the surrender period.

Suppose an age 65 consumer purchased an annuity with a maturity date of age 95 that had a 10 year surrender period. The consumer would probably incur a penalty if the annuity was cashed in before age 76. However, there would be no charge for almost every annuity on the market if the consumer cashed in the policy after the surrender period ended. What about the age 95 maturity date? All this means is the consumer must begin to withdraw money from their annuity at age 95. The maturity date is the longest the consumer can force the insurer to keep the money, not the other way around.

The annuityowner may get off the annuity highway at any exit

Fixed annuities have maturity dates that permit the consumer to keep an annuity until age 85, 95, or even 105. However, saying that this locks you in is like saying if you get on Interstate 80 in New York you can't get off until you reach San Francisco. A fixed annuity is a financial highway, and just like on the Interstate the driver can choose to exit at any time, but they need to be aware of any early tolls.

Or someone will say "an 80 year old should not buy an annuity with a (7, 10, 12, 15) year surrender charge because it ties up their money". The truth in this argument depends on the needs – and not the age – of the annuity owner and the features of the annuity chosen. If the annuity owner will probably need access to most or all of the money before the annuity's surrender period is over then they should buy a different annuity with a shorter surrender period or put less in the annuity. Other concerns can also be met by selecting an annuity with the features needed.

If an annuity owner believes they may need access to more than annual interest down the road then the annuity selected might offer a cumulative penalty-free withdrawal feature. If an annuity owner wishes to make all of the annuity value immediately available upon death, then the annuity chosen should not have any restrictions on payment of death proceeds. If the annuity owner is concerned about possible nursing home bills if future health fades, then the annuity selected should have a nursing home provision permitting access to funds. You can never be too old for the right annuity.

A fixed annuity candidate is not determined by age but by needs and risk tolerance. Put simply, a 75 year old with good genes, sufficient resources, and a high tolerance for risk may never be a fixed annuity candidate because they do not want or need the safety features. On the other hand, an age 30 worker with scads of time until retirement may never develop the emotional tolerance to risk money and would be a good fixed annuity candidate.

Annuity Illusions

You are not going to die May 7, 2044

According to a Society of Actuaries study roughly three-quarters of folks surveyed felt they would live until age 80, but roughly the same percentage thought they would be dead by age 85. I believe the reason for this groupthink, whereby everybody dies in the same five year period, is due to the media talking about life expectancy and the public misunderstanding it.

We keep hearing about our life expectancy being 81.6 years or 83.1 years or such. It appears many people take this to mean that if they are age 48 today that they will die on May 7, 2044 exactly as their lifespan hits age 83.1 years, as if some cosmic actuary pulls the plug on their life cord.

The reality is life expectancy is the point at which half of the people in your particular segment will be dead. This means half will die early – need more life insurance? And half will live longer – that annuity income benefit might be very useful!

One of the reasons that immediate annuities are a hard sale is that the consumer thinks the annuity payout is stacked in the insurance company's favor. The consumer often feels the insurer knows the consumer will die early making the insurance "casino" the big winner.

The odds of dying early can be perceived as less of a gamble if the representative discovers the consumer has a few nonagenarians in the family tree. If the consumer accepts that Dad and Mom lived to age 90 an annuity looks more attractive.

The other approach is to change course. A guaranteed lifetime withdrawal benefit will not provide as high a payout as a life-only annuity, but access to the account balance makes it look like retirement planning and not retirement gambling. Or, an immediate annuity with an installment refund benefit that guarantees to return at least the original principal may make the consumer feel less like a mark.

Hypothetical Returns

Due to onerous rules of disclosure you seldom see hypothetical performance illustrations used with securities, but they are common with fixed annuities.

Hypotheticals Do Not Predict The Future

Whether you are looking at a *Morningstar* or *Value Line* or a *Bookie Bob* track record of historical performance one always needs to be aware that past performance in any shape or form whatsoever has absolutely no bearing, correlation or predictive powers regarding future returns of any financial vehicle.

And yet we all try to use past data to predict future events or look for a modern Cassandra to lead us (and like Cassandra's prophecies if we actually heard the truth we'd probably ignore it).

Hypotheticals based on the past will not tell you what future results will be or the probability of certain results. Even results based on the finest computer models can only tell you the probability of certain outcomes if the model's assumptions are correct. It is like spinning a roulette wheel based on the outcome of a roll of the dice.

And Hypotheticals Do Not Predict The Past

The other problem is most index annuities cannot even predict the past because today's cap rate or participation rate or yield spread can be changed. In the last year alone caps on most products have swung from 25% higher to 25% lower than where they started. Two hypothetical studies looking at the same historical period could post results 50% apart depending upon the day you ran the illustration.

But They Can Help Detect "Too Good" Rates

In the fixed rate world it is easier. If ten products have similar surrender periods, similar guarantees and similar commissions, but one of these products has an initial interest rate that is 2% above all the others, questions would be asked. Index annuities are more difficult to compare because of the wide variety of crediting methods used, and this is where hypothetical models are useful in detecting returns that are outside the norms so that questions can be raised.

Hypothetical models may also be used to verify marketing claims. If a hypothetical model shows an annuity at the current rate never produces a 10% or greater return for the entire surrender period, and the marketer claims their annuity will give consumers "double-digit" returns you have reason to doubt the veracity of the marketer's message.

A hypothetical average annualized return of 6.12% over past 5-year periods does not mean you are likely to earn 6.12% over the next 5-year period. For that to happen the future period would have to exactly repeat as the past did and the participation rates or caps would never change. The hypothetical results have no bearing on future returns, which is probably the most important reality to remember.

Tax Deferral Is Always Worthwhile

If your choice is between a 5-year CD with a rate of, say, 4.35%, or an annuity locking in a rate of 4.05% for five years, why would you choose the annuity? The answer representatives often give is because the annuity offers tax deferral.

Okay. Let us say you are in the 33% combined tax bracket and you put $10,000 into the CD and $10,000 into the annuity. The CD is earning 4.35%, but 33% of that 4.35% – or 1.44% – is lost to taxes, so you really only have 2.91% working for you. A rate of 2.91% compounded on $10,000 produces a balance of $11,542 in 5 years. Interest earned inside the annuity, on the other hand, is not subject to taxes and the full 4.05% goes to work for you. A rate of

4.05% compounded on $10,000 produces a balance of $12,195 in 5 years. At first glance the annuity apparently wins.

5 Year CD		5 Year Annuity
4.35%	Yield	4.05%
-1.44%	Taxes	0%
2.91%	Net Yield	4.05%
$11,542	Balance	$12,195
-0-	Taxes	- 724
$11,542	In Pocket	$11,471

But wait, to make an honest apples-to-apples comparison we should look at the after-tax effect if the annuity is cashed out at the end of the fifth year. We have an annuity balance of $12,195, but $2,195 is interest and subject to our 33% tax rate. A third of $2,195 is $724 in taxes paid, and subtracting $724 in taxes from the $12,195 annuity balance results in cash in hand of $11,471 for the annuity versus $11,542 for the CD. The bank wins this round.

The reality is in this rate environment when looking at a five-year or shorter periods, tax deferral only gets you 5 to 20 basis points of yield. To put this another way, if you are in the 15% tax bracket and the annuity has a rate of, say, 4.00%, if a CD has a rate higher than 4.05% the CD will put more money in your pocket if you cash out in 5 years. If you are in the 33% tax bracket with that same annuity, a CD rate higher than 4.20% will beat the 4.00% annuity on an after-tax basis in 5 years.

And tax-deferral may offer no benefit at all. If you have a couple over age 65 getting, say, $11,000 in Social Security benefits, withdrawing $10,000 from their IRAs and earning $9,000 in taxable bank CD interest for total income of $30,000, the couple is paying zero income taxes because their gross taxable income is offset by the standard deduction and personal exemptions. If anything tax deferral could be creating a future tax liability.

Does this mean buying a CD may result in a better return to the customer than buying an annuity? Yes. There are times when interest yield curves flatten out and CD rates are higher than stated annuity rates.

How do you compete when bank rates are higher? Consumers buy annuities for other reasons besides tax deferral. If someone is on the cusp of being subjected to Social Security benefit taxation, moving money to a deferred annuity may keep their benefits untaxed. If yield is a concern there are annuities with rates linked to external indices that offer a realistic opportunity of out-yielding the bank. Index annuities have been extremely competitive with CD rates over previous 5-year periods. Tax deferral is often a benefit, but you need to look at the whole picture.

> I like tax-deferral because it is usually best to pay a dollar of taxes tomorrow instead of today. I like tax-deferral because it can make investment decisions easier – I can sell a VA growth fund sub-account and move the money to an international fund sub-account without the hassle of calculating and paying taxes, as I would if I sold one mutual fund and bought another. I like tax-deferral because it gives me control over when I declare my interest and pay the taxes. But one should be careful about touting tax-deferral benefits without knowing the financial specifics of the consumer across the table.

Some Annuity Realities

I have listed several financial illusions that sometimes get in the way of the annuity sale and now it is time for some annuity realities. Fixed annuities have a number of great benefits, but they are not perfect.

Liquidity – *Fixed annuity surrender penalties can be as long as 18 years and may result in a consumer getting back as little as 75 cents on the dollar if annuity is cashed in early. Some annuities cannot be cashed in and must be annuitized.*

I do not believe that a 15 year surrender period is too long or a 10 year penalty period is just right. The correct answer is the annuity must meet the liquidity needs of the consumer taking into consideration the consumer's other assets.

Tax Status – *Annuity interest is tax-deferred, not tax-free. Interest is subject to an additional 10% penalty if withdrawn before age 59½. Interest received is always taxed at ordinary income rates, regardless of holding period. There is no step up in account value basis at death.*

The effect of these realities to a large extent depends upon the comparison made.

Pure tax-free municipal bond yields often, but not always, tends to be less than the net after-tax deferral yield of a fixed annuity. Municipal bond interest, unlike tax-deferred interest, is included in calculating Social Security benefit taxation.

Whether the 10% "under age 59½" penalty is a killer depends upon the respective yields. If both Annuity A and Non-Annuity B have a 5% rate, and the owner is under age 59½ and withdrawing the interest, the annuity is effectively giving up half of a percent to the IRS as a tax penalty and netting 4.5%. But what if Annuity A has a 5% rate and Non-Annuity B has a 4.25% rate? Annuity A then wins this heat.

Tax-deferred ordinary income versus capital gains tax treatment is seldom simple. How tax efficient is the taxable choice? Will the Alternative Minimum Tax come into play? Will the ordinary tax rate be higher or lower when tax-deferred interest is received? Depending upon the assumptions used either side can be made to win.

Usually if you are the beneficiary of an annuity your tax basis is the cost of the original owner; if you receive stocks due to a death your tax basis is the fair market value at date of death. The annuity loses this tax battle on an appreciated asset.

No Federal Insurance On Accounts – *Fixed annuities are only backed by company assets, and as a last recourse, state guaranty associations funded by carrier assessments.*

Although some attempt to win this argument by bashing FDIC, you will almost never convince a consumer that a non-federally insured place is safer than a federally insured one. A fixed annuity is not safer than FDIC because by definition federal insurance trumps state guarantees.

The point is not that CDs are unsafe it is that fixed annuities are also safe.

Penalties Often Last Longer Than Current Rates – *A typical fixed annuity may reset some aspect of interest crediting before surrender penalties end, and even policies that have minimum renewal rate factors have them usually set so low the policy would be uncompetitive at the minimum.*

With the exception of multiple year guaranteed rate annuities most annuities involve a "trust me" factor whereby some aspect of the interest credited may change before you can withdraw your accumulated value without penalty. I believe annuities need this flexibility to cope with changing financial conditions, but that doesn't obscure the fact that this flexibility is unilateral.

Opaque Cost Structure – *Sales commissions, policy costs and profitability factors are hidden, and annuity crediting method structures are often opaque, making it impossible for a consumer to truly compare the merits of one annuity with another.*

True.

Math Illusions

The illusion is not in the math. If you plug numbers into any math formula you will get the correct answer based on the numbers used. The illusion is how the answer is presented by some people.

What this section is about is showing what the answers produced by a few common financial formulas are supposed to mean and how these answers are often manipulated..

I believe the reasons so many people seem to be intimidated by math were too many poor math teachers (ones that were good at solving math problems but not necessarily good at teaching math) and a lack of essay questions on math tests (meaning students could not bluff through the math answers and actually needed to study). The problem with not understanding math is others with a little more math savvy may then use math to deceive. What I am going to try to do is talk about some basic financial math, how it can create a false impression, and the additional information you might need to find out the facts.

Mean (Average)

We all know how to figure out the *Average* or *Mean* of a bunch of numbers. You simply add up the numbers, divide the total you get by how many numbers there were, and the result is the average. With the exception of golf scores and the rate of inflation higher averages are usually a good thing.

Say that you were looking at two financial instruments. Instrument A had an average past return of 5% and Instrument B had an average past return of 6%. If you believe the past will exactly repeat which one would you pick? The obvious answer is B because it has a higher average, but sometimes you need to go beyond the average.

A's 6 Numbers: 4%, 4%, 5%, 5%, 6%, 6%

Instrument A has 6 outcomes of which 2 are 4%, 2 are 5% and 2 are 6%. What are the odds of carning 4% if the past returns exactly repeat? 2 out of 6 or 0.33%. There are 6 possible outcomes. There are 2 returns of 4%. Having 2 chances out of 6 possibilities means there is a 33% chance of having a 4% return show up (2/6 = 0.33). Because there are also 2 5% returns and 2 6% returns there is a 2 in 6 or 33% shot of earning either 4% or 5% or 6% with A.

105

B's 6 Numbers: 1%, 1%, 1%, 1%, 6%, 26%

B also has 6 outcomes of which 4 are 1%, 1 is 6% and 1 is 26%. There are 4 chances of earning 1%. If you divide the number of 1% outcomes (4) by the total (6) you get 0.67; if you divide each other outcome (1 chance at 6% and 1 chance at 26%) by the total (6) you get 0.17 for each (0.1667 before rounding). So, based on history, B has a 67% chance, or a 4 out of 6 chance, of producing a 1% return and only a 17% shot (1 in 6 chance) of returning 6% and a 17% shot (1 in 6 chance) of 26% with B.

A's 6 Numbers: 4% +4%+5%+5%+6%+6% = 30/6 = 5%

The average return of A was 5%. From a probability standpoint you have an equal chance of earning 4% or 5% or 6%, so regardless of the outcome you are going to be within one percent of hitting that average return of 5%, and there is a 4 out of 6 chance you will earn at least the average return.

B's 6 Numbers: 1%, 1%, 1%, 1%, 6%, 26% = 36/6 = 6%

The average return of B was 6%, but B has a 4 out of 6 probability you will earn 1%, a 1 in 6 chance you will earn 6% and a 1 in 6 chance you will earn 26%. The probability of earning 6% or greater is only 33% – or a 2 in 6 chance.

Averages can often be misleading because a couple of very high or very low numbers can distort the picture.
You need to go beyond averages.

You will earn at least 4% with A and the odds are pretty good you will earn 5% or 6%. With B the odds are strong you will earn 1% but there is a slim chance of earning 26%. Which is best? The answer depends on your risk tolerance. However, if your main concern was never earning less than 4% A would be the better choice – and you would never know this if you were only told the average.

Standard Deviation

The *Standard Deviation* shows how widely the returns differ (deviate) from the Average. I am not going to show how it is calculated (you can find it in any statistics book) but I want to discuss what it means.

In a normally distributed group of numbers (the population of the sample group) 68% of the results will be within one standard deviation of the Average and 95% will be within two. Here is what that means in our examples:

The Standard Deviation (SD) of the population for Instrument A is 1 (rounded up from 0.9). What that means is roughly two-thirds of the returns fall between Average 5% plus or minus 1 (or between 4% and 6%), and 95% fall between Average 5% ± 1 ± 1 (or between 3% and 7%).

1 SD contains 68% of the possible returns
2 SD contains 95% of the possible returns

The Standard Deviation of the population for Instrument B is 10. What that means is roughly two-thirds of the returns fall between Average 6% plus or minus 10 (or between -4% and 16%), and 95% fall between Average 6% ± 10 ± 10 (or between -14% and 26%).

Without knowing the actual numbers in the group, but knowing only the standard deviation, we can conclude there is a very strong chance (95%) that A would earn somewhere between 3% and 7%; a pretty tight band of returns around that 5% Average. Based on B's Standard Deviation, we have a 95% chance of losing up to 14% or earning up to 26%; a huge return swing from worst to best with each end a long way from B's 6% Average.

The returns of Instrument B are a lot more volatile than those of Instrument A. Using A's standard deviation you are almost certainly going to earn at least 3%; B is much more of a crapshoot (of course, since we know all of the possible outcomes we know the worst we can do is 4% or 1%, but we normally do not know all of the outcomes).

Does this suggest that a low standard deviation is automatically better than a high one? No.

A higher Standard Deviation means more volatility, not better or worse

Suppose a new Instrument C has an Average Return of 4.5% and a standard deviation of only 0.05. This would mean a 95% shot of earning between 4.4% and 4.6% with C. But we know Instrument A has a two-third chance of earning either 5% or 6%, and the worst we could do is earn 4%, which is not all that much lower than the best possible Instrument C return. In a choice between A or C Instrument A will probably produce a better return even though A's standard deviation is higher.

To Sum Up
A lot of folks look only at the average and assume that is pretty much what they are going to earn – and that could be true if the Standard Deviation is low. By comparing the Average and the Standard Deviation, you can get an idea of the range of the returns. If the Standard Deviation is large you may want to look at the actual returns and get an idea of the real top and bottom. A larger standard deviation means more volatility, but it is not an issue of good or bad.

The final comment is all of this analysis only works if the numbers hold true. Consider if we had used degrees on the thermometer instead of percentages and the data represented high daily temperatures during a Minnesota January. All of this data would be worthless if we were trying to use it to predict next summer's temperatures in Duluth.

Compounding versus Simple Interest

The growth in the next year is not just on the original amount (simple interest), it is on the original principal and the interest it earned beyond the principal (compound interest).

Compound returns make it easy to compare returns for different periods. If all of your alternatives were using a five-year period and one produced a 20% return, one a 28% return and one a 30% return, you would select the 30% return, everything else being equal. But what if the 20% return was over 4 years, the 25% was over five years and the 30% was over six years? If you divide the total returns by the respective number of years you get an answer of 5% for all three periods. However, on a compound basis the 4-year return is 4.66%, the 5-year return is 4.56% and the 6-year return is 4.47%. Unless you are comparing results over the same timeframe you cannot get good results by simply dividing the total return by the number of years and picking the highest number.

Compound interest is referred to in many ways: annualized return, internal rate of return (IRR), annual percentage rate (APR), annual percentage yield (APY), but they all mean taking into account the effects of interest on the original amount.

What Does This Mean

If "A" has a higher total return than "B", but "B" had a higher annualized return than "A" then talking only about total return would induce many consumers to choose "A".

If A's annualized return seems low, talking about it as a total return will make it seem higher because many people will simply divide the total by the number of years to determine the return. For example, if A returns 100% over 10 years and B returns 45% over 5 years too many people would conclude that A was better because they would earn 10% a year (100%/10) instead of 9% (45%/5). Of course the reality is A's real annualized return is 7.18% and B produces 7.71%.

Sales Points

> ➤ If the past works against you change the past

> ➤ Make positives seem bigger and negatives seem smaller

> ➤ Misunderstanding the difference between volatility and risk helps fixed annuities

> ➤ Annuities offer an insured retirement alternative

Background Sources

Projection Bias References
John Grable, Ruth Lytton and Barbara O'Neill. 2004. Projection bias and financial risk tolerance. *The Journal of Behavioral Finance.* 5.3:142-147

D. Hirshleifer. 2001. Investor psychology and asset pricing. *Journal of Finance.* 56:1533-1597

H Shefrin. 2000. *Beyond Greed and Fear*. Harvard Business School Press. Boston.

Vividness Bias
Yamagishi, K. 1997. When a 12.86% mortality is more dangerous than 24.14%: Implications for risk communication. *Applied Cognitive Psychology.* 11: 495

Wall Street's Retirement Income Plan
Ameriaks, Veres, Warshawsky. 2001. Making retirement income last a lifetime. *Journal of Financial Planning.* 14;12:66

William F. Sharpe, Jason S. Scott, and John G. Watson. 2007. Efficient retirement financial strategies. *Pension Research Council Working Paper Series.* SSRN: http://ssrn.com/abstract=1005652

Historical Returns & Other Delusions
Bogle, John. 1991. Investing in the 1990s. *The Journal Of Portfolio Management.* Spring

Ianthe Jeanne Dugan. 2004. Sharpe Point: Risk gauge is misused. *The Wall Street Journal.* 31 August. C1

Jeremy Siegel. 1992. The equity premium: Stock and bond returns since 1802. *Financial Analysts Journal.* 48; 1:28

Dark Illusions – Bogus Names & Inexperts
Cooper, Gulen, Rau. 2005. Changing names with style. *The Journal Of Finance.* 60.6:2825

Torngren & Montgomery. 2004. Worse than chance? performance and confidence among professionals and laypeople in the Stock market. *The Journal of Behavioral Finance.* 5.3:148

Johnson et al. 1993. Framing, probability distortions and insurance uncertainty, *Journal of Risk and Uncertainty.* 7.1:35-51

Johnson & Goldstein. 2003. Do defaults save lives? *Center for Decision Sciences.* Columbia University

Annuity Myths From Wall Street
Koco, Linda. 2002. Retirement income studies point up opportunities for insurers, brokers. *National Underwriter.* 106.27:12

Annuity Illusions
Society Of Actuaries. 2006. *Key Findings and Issues Longevity: The Underlying Driver of Retirement Risk 2005 Risks and Process of Retirement Survey Report.* July

Chapter 5 – Consumer Behavior

You have all been there. You perfectly explained the rational reasons why the annuity makes sense, you have corrected the consumer on a couple of illusions they held on how annuities work and they seem to accept your answers. The consumer has the money and the need for your annuity solution, and yet they still do not buy.

What this chapter is about are the behavioral reasons that influence decisions and what the representative can do about them. What it does is describe the behavior, show an example or two or three of the behavior screwing up the sale, and then offer ways to counter the behavior, if needed. These are behaviors that often result in no sale, but when the representative knows about them and sees them in use they can remember solutions from this chapter to counter the bad decision and influence the good decision, which is to buy the annuity.

In naming the behaviors I have used the most commonly recognized name. A behavior may have more than one name because different researchers worked on identifying the same behavior in different studies and developed separate names for the same thing. As a practical matter there is no reason to know the academic names at all. Instead of "regret aversion" I could have made up some name because the importance is not in knowing the name of the psychological action that is hampering the sale, it is figuring out how to work with or around it to close the sale. I left the academic name in, and sometimes list relevant articles, just in case the reader wants to do more research on a certain behavior. But this chapter is not about research and it is not about academics. This chapter is about understanding the behaviors that can get in the way of the sale so that you remove them and make the sale.

Projection Bias (Naive Extrapolation)

I talked about this in the chapter on illusions, but it also exerts a direct and irrational influence on behavior. What projection bias means is taking what happened yesterday and today and making decisions based on it happening tomorrow. What is does is cause consumers to react emotionally when making decisions, and this often hurts them. The following is a real-life example of projection bias peril.

<u>Stock Market Folly</u>

It is interesting to compare money going into the stock market with the coinciding movements of the stock market. This chart covers a timeframe from the beginning of 1996 though the end of 2003 using data from the Investment Company Institute *Trends In Mutual Fund Investing*. The period includes the great bull market of the '90s as well as the millennium bear market that followed. The red line shows money going into or coming out of equity mutual funds. The blue line shows the value of the S&P 500 index.

3 Month Rolling Average

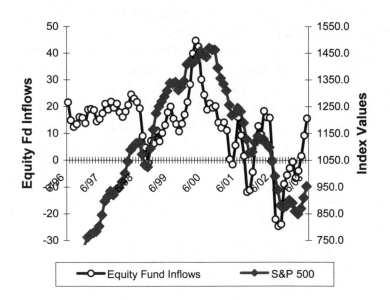

As you can see, for 1996, 1997 and the first half of 1998 the money going into mutual funds each month remained relatively constant. Even though the S&P 500 soared from around 750 to over 1100 the level of money put into mutual funds each month remained level. It looked like investors finally had that dollar-cost-averaging strategy down to a science and were not succumbing to irrational exuberance.

In the summer of 1998 the stock market was hit with three whammies. First, the Asian economies experienced a banking crisis, then the Russian government decided not to pay off on their own bonds, and the United States faced the impeachment of a president. The reaction to all of this was a hundred-point drop in the index, but the market quickly shrugged off the bad news and was back to setting records in a couple of months. What was the reaction of mutual fund investors?

They quit buying mutual funds. And even as the index swept upwards past 1100, 1200, 1300 they put less money into mutual funds than they had in the past. It was not until the index passed the 1350 mark that investors began buying mutual funds in earnest, at which time they began buying funds in record amounts. And they kept buying funds in record amounts as the index went past 1450 and then declined to 1350, then 1250, then 1150 and 1050. In fact, they did not begin to sell mutual funds until the index dropped to 850, at which time they sold mutual funds in record amounts – which coincided with the lowest point of the millennium bear market.

If you were ever looking for a real world example of the maxim "buy high – sell low" this is it. Investors bought when the stock market was at its highest points and sold when it was at its lowest. Why? Why did investors retreat from the market when it was a good time to buy, but keep throwing good money after bad when the market was in a downward spin? The reason is they took what was happening in the past and projected it forward.

Hindsight Bias

It took months to get my Dad out of some CDs to buy a 10 year Treasury with a 15% coupon back in 1981 because he knew interest rates would keep rising forever (projection bias is everywhere). After I had pushed him into buying the 15% Treasury, and he watched CD rates tumble down and down, he was fond of regaling me of *his* wise decision to buy Treasuries because it showed how smart he was about financial markets.

Hindsight Bias makes us think we are smarter than we really are.

Hindsight bias observes that people are smarter after the outcome of the decision has been observed. If the decision was a good one people go back and change the memory of their events of the decision to believe they knew it would be a good decision and that is why they made it, and if it was a bad decision they find external justification to show why they were misled into a making a bad decision that obviously was not their fault.

116

Not Learning From A Near-Miss

The representative pleaded with the consumer to pull back from the stock market, sell today and pocket those gains, and place at least some money in a no-market-risk place. Reluctantly the consumer took the representative's advice, got out of the market and bought the annuity. And just as predicted, the stock market dropped like a rock. If the consumer had not listened to the agent they would have lost half of their money!

Is the consumer more or less likely to get back in the stock market?
The answer is more likely. And the reason is a mental illusion we play on ourselves called hindsight bias.

After the near-miss of a disaster we tell ourselves that we "knew what was going to happen all along." The representative is forgotten and the consumer becomes the hero in their own mind. In hindsight, the consumer sees all the things that pointed to a stock market decline and justifies why the decision was made. And because the outcome of the decision was favorable the consumer's invulnerability is reinforced. The problem is it will be harder for the representative to convince the consumer the next time the market may head down because the consumer believes avoiding the last near-miss proved their predictive I-can-do-no-wrong powers.

What can the representative do?
Remind the consumer that the representative played a major role in the consumer's decision.

117

Emphasize what a close call it was and ask if the consumer really wants to tempt fate again.

What if the consumer did not listen and was hit by the drop?
Hindsight bias also means if the consumer made a bad decision they will find external justification to show why they were misled into a making a bad decision that obviously was not their fault. Naturally the stock market loss was due to the last advisor, which is why the consumer needs a new representative.

Regret Aversion
Regret Aversion assumes people experience regret and joy, and when making decisions when the outcome is not clear we try to anticipate and deal with these feelings. What that means is we try to do things that we believe will not cause us regret.

Regret Aversion 1 – Let Losses Run
If it might be best for a consumer to move some of their money out of a security and into a fixed annuity, would it be best to approach the consumer A) when they are up and have gained 10% on their security investment, or B) when they are down and have lost 10% on their investment.

The answer is A. Index annuities protect consumers from stock market loss, so it would seem logical that consumers might be more receptive to moving money into index annuities after a market decline. After all, they have experienced a loss in their investment so the appeal of a no-market-risk instrument should be even greater. Although the logic is sound it conflicts with the emotional response known as regret aversion. To avoid regret we do not want to admit we made the wrong economic decision.

When a consumer sells an investment for less than they paid the consumer is admitting he or she made a bad decision, and what is even worse than admitting the bad decision is the feeling that the investment may eventually go back up in value and be a winner thus proving they were originally right. Regret aversion explains why investors tend to hold on to losing stocks. It also explains why folks sell winning stocks too soon. If you sell a stock and take a profit you validate your original decision – you picked a stock and it went up. It may still go up higher, but you know that regardless of what happens down the road that you are a winner today.

What this may mean for representatives is that the best time to approach a consumer with the annuity story is after the consumer has made some money in the market and not after they have lost money. If they leave the market with a gain the consumer gets out of the stock market and into the annuity feeling like a winner with the knowledge that the annuity will never be a loser.

Regret Aversion 2 – Guaranteed Gains & Gamble On Losses
You are given a) 50/50 choice between earning 12% or getting 0% or b) getting a guaranteed 6%. Which do you choose? Or, you have already earned 12%. You are given a choice between a) automatically losing 3% and winding up with 9% or b) a 50/50 choice between keeping 12% or winding up with a 6% return. Which do you choose?

50/50 odds of 12% Gain or 0% Gain OR Guaranteed Gain of 6%

Guaranteed Loss of 3% OR **50/50 odds of 6% Loss or 0% Loss**

From a rational economic point of view a consumer would either take the 50/50 choice each time or the guarantee each time, because that would be consistent; however, most consumers choose b) in both cases – guarantee the gain and take a chance on the loss.

When it comes to gains people like certainty. I believe a big factor limiting index annuity sales is that the typical annuity prospect is choosing between the sure thing of the stated bank rate and the uncertainty of an index-linked yield. These consumers are averse to losing the sure thing they already have. However, they will consider the "gamble" if either the payoff is high enough or they feel the odds of earning more than the bank will pay are in their favor.

This explains why index annuity sales soar when one-year CD rates drop to 2% and tend to flatten when CD rates rise to 5%. It also explains why index annuities with interest caps meet with increasing resistance as the gap between bank rates and maximum cap interest narrows.

Since the representative cannot control what interest the bank pays what can be done when CD rates go up? If bank rates are high pick an index annuity with a high potential payoff. If a consumer can get 5% on a CD and the potential interest on the index annuity next year is anywhere from 0% to 7% (due to a cap), the consumer will feel there simply isn't enough payoff to justify the gamble. However, if an annuity without a cap was presented, the consumer may feel the odds are right. The consumer needs to feel that the potential payoff is at least double what the bank is paying if one of the potential payoffs is zero.

Another method is to challenge the odds; if a consumer feels strongly the index will go up in the future they may accept a smaller differential between the sure thing and the index-linked interest. A possible 7% probably would not induce someone to give up a guaranteed 5%, unless they felt the 7% was a sure thing.

The uncertainty of the future interest earned is what keeps many people from buying index annuities. Consumers need to be educated on the rational reasons why the index annuity is not a gamble.

A strong advantage fixed annuities do possess is no downside market risk. A consumer should be reminded that with a fixed annuity they will never be forced to choose between a sure loss or the risk of a loss.

Regret Aversion 3 – Do Nothing

In the near term we regret doing <u>something</u>, but in the long term we regret doing <u>nothing</u>. If we have a choice of not making a change it causes us less mental turmoil today to simply do nothing. The problem is when we look back at the situation we often regret that we did not make the change.

One way to deal with this is to try to put the consumer into the future, but acknowledge the turmoil today. It would be saying, "I understand it is difficult to try something new, but picture yourself looking back one year from now. Could you look back with a clear conscience and tell yourself not getting the annuity benefit was the best decision?"

Regret Aversion: What Can Be Done
I will give you more ways to overcome regret aversion problems in the chapter on framing.

Loss Aversion

Loss Aversion (also called Myopic Loss Aversion) means that losses hurt more than gains – that losing a dollar brings us greater sorrow than gaining a dollar brings in joy. Some studies have found that losses hurt twice as much as gains.

Losses hurt twice as much as gains

In the Regret Aversion example I said that people are less likely to move if they have a loss rather than a gain, but this reaction ends when the perception of loss becomes big enough. A clear example of this is in the Projection Bias section that talked about investors not selling at the start of the millennium bear market but getting out of the market at the bottom of the cycle. The reason is the investors went from regret – I do not want to recognize my mistake, to fear – my mistake will cause me greater loss. Their aversion to loss became greater than their regret of being initially wrong and their projection bias made these losses go into the future.

Loss aversion can be tough to counter because it is driven strongly by fear. In the annuity world an answer is to show that certain losses – like losses due to a down stock market – cannot occur. Another solution is to show the potential gain is greater than the possible loss "this annuity yields twice as much interest as the CD and the risk of the insurance company going under is very remote."

Loss Aversion: What Can Be Done

Proper framing helps to minimize the effects of Loss Aversion, but Loss Aversion exerts a strong emotional pull on our decisions. You need to show the possible gain as greater than the possible loss – a 50/50 proposition is not enough.

You may also need to make the potential loss seem more manageable, perhaps by going for a smaller sale or offering an annuity with a *return of premium feature* that allows the contract to be cashed in without surrender penalties.

Choice Conflict (Choice Overload)

Your old 401(k) plan had two choices – a bond account and a stock account. Your new 401(k) plan offers four bond strategies and fourteen equity accounts. The new plan makes you a) more likely to contribute or b) less likely.

The answer is b). The more choices a consumer is offered the more likely it is that the consumer will do nothing. This is because of an economic behavior known as Choice Conflict or Choice

Overload. It is a form of Regret Aversion in that the more choices consumers are offered the greater the fear of making a wrong decision, so the consumer elects not to make a decision.

A CD or a fixed rate annuity decision tree has limited branches – you either buy today or you do not. However, index annuities come in a rainbow of alternatives. Unfortunately, studies have shown that the more choices you give a person the less likely they are to make a decision.

Not: Choose One From Each Column		Instead
APP	S&P 500	*"You could put half into*
Averaging	Dow Jones	*the S&P 500 using*
Cap Forward	Bond Index	*averaging and half into*
Trigger	Nikkei 225	*Bond Index"*
Yield Spread	Nasdaq	

Instead of overloading the consumer with choices an index annuity can often be presented as a "would you like this or that" decision. The consumer should be presented with a "prepackaged" solution that minimizes conflict. Instead of asking the consumer how the premium should be split up amongst the six crediting methods and the four indices, the consumer could be presented with a solution of 50% of their money in Index A with Method X and 50% in Index B and Method Y. Of course, the consumer is always free to make their own choices.

It is important to remember that the basic design of fixed annuities already limits potential conflict; the choice is not between a) making money or b) losing money, it is between a) making some money and b) making more money, and that's rewarding a good choice.

Choice Conflict: What Can Be Done

If there are multiple options the consumer should be presented with simple suggested or packaged solutions to avoid choice overload. But there is a time when choice should be increased.

Say a consumer asks what the minimum required premium is. If the representative says it is $10,000 the consumer may only buy $10,000. If the representative says $10,000 but the consumer gets an interest bonus at $100,000, some consumers will buy $100,000 but most will still buy $10,000. However, if the representative says $10,000, and there is an interest bonus at $100,000, but the usual purchase is $35,000, more consumers will buy $35,000.

It is the same reason restaurants offer small, medium and large drinks. We do not like to think of ourselves as small minded, we may feel large is overdoing it, but medium seems just right.

Hedonic Editing (House Money)

You are walking back to the hotel from the casino with $500 of the casino's money in your pocket. You pass by a jeweler's window displaying a $300 ring that really strikes your fancy. Or, you pass by the same jeweler having lost $500 at the casino. Assuming $500 is not a life-changing sum are you more likely to buy the ring if you a) had won at the casino or b) had lost.

Most folks would be more likely to buy the ring if they had won at the casino because they would feel they were buying it with "house money" and not their own. After a consumer realizes a gain subsequent expenses will, at least for awhile, be seen as coming from part of the gain. In gambling circles it is known as playing with house money, in behavioral economic theory it is known as Hedonic Editing. The feeling is not permanent; by the next morning that $500 in our wallet becomes normal money, but for the moment the $500 is not subject to the normal rationalizations we make with money and may be spent without guilt. And this bit of economic behavior can be used to help sell insurance products.

House Money

"I now have $2,000 more"

If one tries to sell a consumer a long-term-care or life insurance policy with a $2,000 premium the consumer's rational mind says that the $2,000 is a cost. However, what if the premium cost is viewed in the context of a $100,000 certificate of deposit that was earning 3% or $3,000 in interest that you moved to a fixed annuity paying 5% or $5,000. If the insurance is pitched and packaged with the annuity purchase the consumer may see the combined event as keeping the original $3,000 interest and getting the $2,000 insurance premium paid for from "house money."

The same concept can be used with tax deferral. For someone with a 25% tax rate turning $8,000 of taxable interest into tax-deferred interest creates a $2,000 tax savings. This savings may even be directly realized by reducing the size of the quarterly estimated IRS income tax payments the consumer is making. Even though tax-deferred interest is not tax free the tax savings are paying for insurance protection needed today.

This has to be presented quickly as a "joint" deal. In a very short time the "house" money turns mentally into "their" money and the insurance once again becomes a cost rather than a freebee.

Hedonic Editing 2- Gain & Loss Shifting
Hedonic editing may also shift the perception of actual gains and losses. For example, say 3 investments each lost 7% and another 3 investments each gained 7%. Although the reality is no

125

gain-no loss, if a consumer was told they lost 21%, but they gained 7 % on "A", 7% on "B" and an additional 7% on "C" they subconsciously feel they've had 3 winners to 1 loser.

7%+7%+7% seems like more than 21%

This concept may be used when presenting fees. An annuity might charge 0.6% for a withdrawal benefit, 0.2% for a death benefit, and 0.2% for a long term care benefit. If the "benefit package" is presented as "you get guaranteed withdrawals, an enhanced death benefit and long term care all for 1%" the editing makes us feel like we are getting 3 benefits for the price of 1.

Hedonic Editing 3 – Distorted Memories

Hedonic editing integrates past events to produce a memory that maximizes happiness. One type of this is the power of positive thinking that salespeople often use where they motivate themselves by remembering the big sale resulting from yesterday's calls, but not the 30 rejections they also received.

Is it bad to put a positive spin on the past? It depends on the action it produces. If hedonic editing causes the salesperson to make another round of calls to suffer through the rejections to get another sale to feed the family, then the editing is probably a good thing because it enables the salesperson to function. However, if the editing said the reason for success was snorting the six lines of cocaine before making the calls – and conveniently forgetting about the downside of cocaine use – then hedonic editing is not a good thing.

Even though hedonic editing causes people to try to find the sunny side of life, when it is needed, consumer tend to be realistic and essentially honest in evaluating their past.

Hedonic Editing: What Can Be Done

If desired, the representative can create the house money effect by separating and quantifying the financial gain produced. We saw where "house money" might be used to create the cash for another insurance purchase, but the effect may also be used to "reward" the consumer for buying the annuity. As an example, the consumer may want to take a trip or buy new furniture, but feels guilty about spending the money. If the annuity creates $2000 in new money the consumer can spend this because it is not coming out of yesterday's wallet.

Separating points makes the total effect seem greater, bundling points makes the total effect seem lesser.

Hedonic editing of memories is fine, as long as it does not keep the consumer from benefiting now. A consumer may remember buying gold in 1983 as a good decision because the price is so much higher today and not want to buy an annuity. The representative should illustrate that the price of gold was flat for 20 years and perhaps an annuity makes sense for the next 20 years.

Endowment Effect

The Endowment Effect is always at work when you are trying to get a consumer to swap what they have – money or an existing annuity – for another annuity. The endowment effect makes us overvalue what we already have over something new. It is the old "a bird in the hand is worth two in the bush" story and it makes us place an unrealistic value on something simply because we own it.

The only real counter for it is to make the consumer believe what you offer is more valuable than what they have, and you do that by directly comparing what the consumer has with what they could own. The Endowment Effect can be defeated by the Ben Franklin close where you list benefits and go with the list that is longer.

127

CD	Annuity
Compound Interest	Compound Interest
Free from Market Risk	Free from Market Risk
Ability to Bypass Probate	Ability to Bypass Probate
	Tax Control
	Minimum Interest Rate
	Guaranteed Lifetime Income
	Tax Deferral
	Avoid Social Security Benefit Taxes

A variation on this is to make the consumer feel they have last year's model. It would be along the lines of the representative saying "Yes, you have a very nice CD; it is what people used to put their money into before they discovered the tax-deferral benefit of annuities" or "your current annuity was state of the art back at the turn of the century, but now annuities come with living benefits".

> **Endowment Effect: What Can Be Done**
> The advantage is knowing it exists and it will make the consumer place an irrationally higher value on what they already own. You defeat the effect by rationally demonstrating that your solution has a higher value, so the consumer can "trade up".

Mood Shaping

A person's emotional state influences how they make decisions of trust about unrelated things. As an example, say the next person coming in your door wants your approval on something. How you respond to their pitch is dramatically affected by whether you just received a call telling you A) your car was sideswiped in the parking lot or B) you won the office Super Bowl pool. The pitch will more likely be accepted if you won the pool, even though it is unrelated to the request. Studies have found that happy participants were more trusting than sad participants, and that sad participants were more trusting than angry participants.

This is not surprising. We are all aware that having a good day or a bad one affects our decisions in general. What research shows is how easy it is to put people in a more trusting frame of mind and how easy it is to counteract the manipulation.

By sharing a positive story or telling an uplifting tale the listener becomes more trusting. Good salespeople intuitively know this and often open with a joke or humorous story, and research shows it works. A sale may result not based on the merits of the solution offered, but because the "trust judgment" has been altered.

But we can neuter the manipulation if we are aware of it. If we hear a funny story, our judgment will not be affected if we consciously think "I'm being told this story to make me more receptive." If we recognize or anticipate the manipulation its power melts away.

What this means is one needs to recognize the emotional state of the other party. If they seem angry or sad the best choice is to delay forcing their decision until another time. If that cannot be done, then the alternative is to make them aware of the real reason they are angry or sad, because this will help to separate the emotion from the decision.

But don't try this with your spouse. Research indicates this emotional manipulation only worked with people we don't know very well, because when people know the real you they have already formed a trust judgment.

Availability Bias

Which is more likely – dying from being struck by lightning or dying in a flood? If you are reading this in the spring of the year you probably said dying in a flood, because when floods occur they tend to get quite a bit of press coverage, but if I asked you during a summer electrical storm you would probably say lightning will kill you. Availability Bias means we give more credibility to things we remember first. However, the first thing to come to mind

129

is not always the best answer. In this instance the National Safety Council reports that the odds of dying in any given year by being struck by lightning is 1 in 6 million while the odds of drowning in a flood are 1 in 13 million (www.nsc.org).

If you are presenting an annuity and mention safety a typical client may immediately think of CDs, if you mention growth the consumer may think of mutual fund, and their feelings about the first thing they think of will influence how they react to the annuity presented.

<u>Show The Consumer Why They Should Change</u>

Related to availability bias is *Familiarity Bias*, which simply means we prefer what we are used to. The representative needs to give the consumer a good reason to choose the unfamiliar. Obvious reasons are the potential for a better yield or greater safety or better features, and any of these reasons provide the extra value needed to justify why the consumer should not stick with the status quo.

Availability Bias: What Can Be Done

The representative needs to be aware of what the consumer may first recall. If the news headlines for the last month have been talking about loss and financial risk the representative will need to begin the talk emphasizing the safety of the annuity they are presenting. If the headlines are screaming stock market gains, talking about either the potential upside of the annuity or how the annuity acts as a balance to the gains and accompanying risk of the market will enable the representative to counter the bias.

Status Quo Bias

This bias ties in with the endowment effect, availability bias and regret aversion. It means sticking with what we have done in the past and simply repeating the same decision, even if we know it is not the best decision (better the devil you know).

It also means we try to avoid finding out how well the alternatives we did not choose perform because they would indicate we made a bad decision. This is known as *Confirmation Bias* and means people search for information that supports their current beliefs and decisions, while neglecting information that might say they are wrong.

A consumer may select the certificate of deposit over the annuity simply because they have owned CDs in the past and the annuity is a new thing. The consumer may even believe the annuity could offer a higher yield, but the consumer minimizes potential regret by telling themselves that even if the annuity beats the CD they will never know and ignorance is bliss.

What does this mean for a representative? Take away their bliss. Research indicates that if the consumer is told they will know the outcome of the alternative not chosen that it will cause them to rethink their decision. What this means is if the consumer is leaning towards the CD and the representative basically says, "If you choose the CD I'll call you in a year and let you know how you would have done in the annuity" that the consumer will be less likely to simply repeat the past decision of buying the CD and will give the index annuity a fair chance.

Gambler's Fallacy & Hot Hands

Both the Gambler's Fallacy and Hot Hands take a small set of results and attempt to use it to predict near-term outcomes, but in opposite directions. Say that you flipped a (fair) coin 5 times and it always came up heads. The Gambler's Fallacy says you would believe that on the next flip tails were "due" so you would say the odds of heads on the next flip are less than 50/50. Hot Hands followers believe in streaks. If the coin turned up heads 5 times in a row a Hot Hands player would say the odds of heads on the next flip are better than 50/50 because a streak is happening. Both are wrong. The odds of every flip on a two-faced (fair) coin are always

50/50, and if you flipped the coin enough times it would balance out.

Mental Accounting

This means we subjectively treat some economic outcomes differently from others without a rational basis for doing so. It explains why we are more likely to sell our good investments and keep the bad ones, cause us not to diversify, and often involves taking the advice of the body parts without brain cells (as in "my heart/gut tells me I should..."). By understanding how mental accounting works a representative can take advantage of it.

Mental Accounting 1 – Goal Pyramid

If you look at a typical financial pyramid offered by Wall Street it shows a bottom level of cash or bonds, a middle level of growth & income mutual funds, and a top of riskier growth investments. Consumers also create pyramids, but a personal pyramid based on goals and fears, not asset classes, and the levels are produced by

132

Mental Accounting. For example, the main goal covering the base of the pyramid might be to produce enough retirement income. The middle goal might be to leave some money for the children, and the "wish" goal might be to leave a significant amount to charity or to buy a tropical vacation home. The way consumers typically allocate is to satisfy the base goal, then reach the middle goals, and if there is still money leftover to try to reach the wish goal. Where consumers are on this personal pyramid and their risk level determines what they invest in, and how the annuity should be presented.

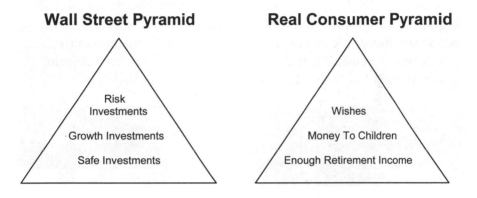

A consumer near or in retirement may still be trying to achieve the goal of having enough retirement income and their risk tolerance might be telling them to preserve what they have. For this consumer fixed annuities can solve two issues – one is the lack of market risk to principal helps the preservation of dollars risk and second the life income made available by guaranteed lifetime withdrawal benefit or annuitization helps the preservation of income risk.

Another consumer near or in retirement may still be trying to achieve the goal of having enough retirement income, but their risk tolerance might be telling them to grow what they have for more future income. This is the type of consumer Wall Street is going after with its targeted mutual funds, stock/bond age-determined allocation and variable annuities with guaranteed accumulation benefits. These consumers feel a fixed annuity does not offer the risk/reward potential of investments and they will continue to own securities to satisfy the growth need. However, for these consumers a fixed annuity may be used as a substitute for the bond component of the asset allocation model.

The consumer is operating in all three goal levels at the same time, and each goal level may have its own risk aversion level that will affect what is selected. For example, a consumer may be very risk averse and choose only fixed annuities for their retirement income goals, but because the chance of leaving a meaningful amount of money to charity is so low they may choose a high risk-high potential reward investment to try to make this goal. Or, the consumer more risk-oriented with their own retirement money might want to ensure that their children receive at least a certain sum and might choose fixed annuities to provide this certainty.

Goal Pyramids: What Can Be Done
Even if the consumer says they are already set for retirement by using securities and are not sufficiently risk-averse to want fixed annuities, they may still need annuities to provide for other goals.

Mental Accounting 2 – Not Understanding Time
We understand that $1 in hand today is worth more than $1 promised to us tomorrow, but we do not act as if $1 received in 11 years is worth more than a dollar received in 12 years. In the short term consumers understand the present value of money versus the future value of money. They may not forgo $1 today to get back $1.10 in a month. However, consumers lose perspective as time increases. The consumer that would not trade $1 today for $1.10 in a month would probably prefer receiving $1.10 in 12 years and one month to getting $1 in 12 years, even though the time difference is the same one month.

The other time perception problem is long-term investments are evaluated based on their short-term returns. If you have a 30 year horizon does it matter how the investments did last quarter? No, but whether our time horizon is 1 year or 30 years we tend to manage our money for the next quarter, and this causes losses to have undue influence on the planning.

Mental Accounting 3 – Sunk Cost
If you have ever held onto a car too long you have probably experienced the bias of sunk cost. Last month you spent $800 fixing the transmission and now it looks like it will need a valve

135

job for another $1200. You know you should sell the car – but last month you put $800 into it (which means you should have sold it before you fixed the transmission). So, do you throw good money after bad or make a fresh start?

You often see this in the investment world where an investor will "average down" and buy more of a doggy stock rather than admit the loss, sell, and move on. You will even see it with CD owners when they attempt to rationalize why they kept long-term money in short-term CDs and thus lost thousands of dollars of higher interest income.

One reason we hold onto inferior decisions is we do not like admitting we made an inferior choice in the first place – it is a type of regret aversion. To protect egos show the consumer that circumstances have changed from when the original purchase was made so they can feel they made the right decisions previously and now it is time to make another right decision. "You were smart to lock in a good rate when you bought the CD but now that the rate environment has changed the multi-year annuity is the right choice" or "It was smart to buy that fixed rate annuity to get that high minimum guarantee because index annuities with GLWBs were not around back then, but the new and improved annuity is now available."

Sunk Cost: What Can Be Done

First, assure the consumer that the old decision was right when they made it, but circumstances have changed and now the representative's solution is the right decision for today. If the consumer is still resisting ask them if they did not own the CD, mutual fund, 78 Plymouth, would they buy it today? Talk about how easy it is to make the change to today's correct solution.

Sales Points

➢ If there are multiple options the consumer should be presented with simple suggested or packaged solutions to avoid choice overload

➢ To get a consumer to make a new decision that conflicts with an old one assure the consumer that the old decision was right when they made it, but circumstances have changed and now the representative's solution is the right decision for today

Background Sources

Hindsight Bias
Blank, H, J. Musch, R. Pohl. 2007. Hindsight bias: on being wise after the event. *Social Cognition. 25.* 1: 1-9

Dillon, R., C. Tinsley. 2008. How near-misses influence decision making under risk. *Management Science.* 54.8:1425–1440

Regret Aversion References
Tversky, Amos, Daniel Kahneman. 1979. Prospect theory: An analysis of ecision under risk. *Econometrica.* 47.2:263-289

Tversky, Amos, Daniel Kahneman. 1986. Rational choice and the framing of decisions. *The Journal of Business.* 59.4:4-12

Bell, David Bell. 1983. Risk premiums for decision regret. *Management Science.* 29.10:1156

Loomes, Graham, Robert Sugden. 1982. Regret theory. *The Economic Journal.* 92:820

Choice Conflict References
Simonson, Carmon, and O'Curry. 1994. Experimental evidence on

the negative effect of product features and sales promotions on brand choice. *Marketing Scienc*e. 13. Winter. 23–40.

Thompson, Hamilton, Trust. 2005. Feature fatigue. *Journal of Marketing Research.* 42.11:431-442

Hedonic Editing
Cowley, Elizabeth. 2008. The perils of hedonic editing. *Journal Of Consumer Research.* 35:71

Thaler, Richard, Johnson, Eric J. 1990, Gambling with the house money and trying to break even, *Management Science.* 36.6: 643

Status Quo Bias & The Endowment Effect
Zeelenberg, Marcel etal. 1996. Consequences of regret aversion. *Organizational Behavior And Human Decision Processes.* 65.2:148–158

Kahneman, Daniel, Jack L Knetsch, Richard H Thaler. 1991. Anomalies The endowment effect, loss aversion, and status quo bias. *The Journal of Economic Perspectives.* 5.1:193

Mood Shaping
Dunn, Jennifer, Maurice E Schweitzer. 2005. Feeling and believing: The influence of emotion on trust. *Journal of Personality and Social Psychology.* 88.5:736

Gambler's Fallacy & Hot Hands
Sundali1, James, Rachel Croson. 2006. Biases in casino betting. *Judgment and Decision Making.* 1:1:1-12.

Mental Accounting
Statman, Meir, Vincent Wood. 2004. Investment temperament. *Journal of Investment Consulting.* April.

Statman, Meir, Hersh Shefrin 2000. Behavioral portfolio theory. *Journal Of Financial And Quantitative Analysis.* 35.2:127-150

Chapter 6 – Framing

Framing is presenting a picture, concept, or fact in a certain way. All of the topics mentioned in this book are examples of framing because framing is a conscious or unconscious way of offering information. We use framing to attempt to explain what something is and how it works relative to something else. Framing is not bad or good, it just is. The representative needs to use framing to their advantage, and be aware when it is working against them.

I have found one of the big reasons why an annuity sale does not happen is because the consumer is anchored in their own financial reality and not in the representative's financial reality. Consumers' heads are rarely anchored in the representative's financial pond, but are in their own separate pond. If the consumer remains in their pond while the representative stays in theirs, the representative does not connect with the consumer and a sale does not happen. What the representative needs to do is move the consumer's anchor into the representative's pond, and this is done by framing.

Framing is used to make the consumer's reality the same as the representative's reality. This chapter shows situations where the consumer's financial reality may interfere with the annuity sale, and tells how to frame the reality so a sale will result.

Setting Up The Sale

Mimicking & Mirroring
Primates tend to mimic the behavior of the primates sitting across from them (monkey see, monkey do). If the other person is smiling, we tend to smile. If the other person is making hand gestures, we will tend to make similar gestures. If the mimicry is positive (returning a smile and not returning a glare) the person being mimicked feels closer to the other person and develops

feelings of rapport and bonding. If a representative mimics the consumer it can help close the sale by making the consumer feel closer to the representative and causing the consumer to want to help the representative.

The Consumer Anchor

This behavioral response is becoming so well known that there have been some articles "warning" consumers that the representative may attempt mimicking during the sales process so that the consumer can be on their guard. However, even when warned about possible mimicking roughly 90% of consumers still do not catch on to what is happening. Even those who catch on still develop the bonding feelings that are caused by mimicking.

The Frame

The representative needs to adopt the body language of the consumer. If the consumer is slouchy the representative should slouch, if the consumer crosses their legs so should the representative. But if the consumer tilts their head to the left the representative would tilt their head to the right (mirroring is when the mimicker does the same action on the opposite side of the body). The representative should not act like a mime by instantly aping everything the consumer does, but subtly adjust to the consumer's movements.

Do Parrot Not Paraphrase

Some of the research contradicts what is traditionally taught in sales training. I remember sales training books saying you should not parrot back what the consumer says, but should instead paraphrase their comments. So, if the consumer says, "I do not like risky investments," the old sales training books suggest the representative says something like, "You are saying you prefer more conservative instruments." However, mimicking research suggests the best representative response is, "You are saying you do not like risky investments?"

Mimicking was even more effective when the consumer knew the representative was biased towards what they were offering. For example, if the representative begins the presentation by saying "I am completely impartial as to the fixed annuity you may select" they would be less effective than if they said, "I am one of the leading representative for XYZ annuities." When the "biased" representative engaged in mimicking behavior the consumer went to greater lengths to help the representative sell them the XYZ annuity because the consumer mimics the positive attitude the representative has.

Superstition
One out of eleven Americans has an unreasonable fear of Friday the 13th, but many consider the number seven to be lucky. In the Chinese culture, the number eight and the color red are considered lucky and the number four and the color black are thought to be unlucky. We know that superstitions are irrational beliefs, and yet they still influence and sometimes overpower rational decision making. People are more likely to rely on a superstitious belief as the uncertainty about the outcome increases.

A study done at an eastern college asked students to place bets on a day that was not Friday the 13th. The bets were they could receive $18 or opt for a one in five chance to win $240 (a four in five chance of getting zero). One group of students was reminded the date was Tuesday the 19th and asked to place their bets. The second group was reminded it was not Friday the 13th and asked to place their bets. Twice as many students in the group that were reminded of Friday the 13th choose the lower risk-much lower payoff of $18 than did the students that were told it was the 19th.

The implication is if the representative is offering a product with a more certain outcome than a competitor's product they might appeal to paraskevidekatriaphobics by saying something like "It's a good thing it's not Friday the 13th" because the consumer would be more likely to choose the multi-year rate guaranteed annuity over the fluctuating index-linked rate certificate of deposit.

141

Superstitious selling also means being aware of cultural superstitions. An annuity with a 12% or 14% bonus will not negatively impact Swedish-American or French-American community's subconscious but one with a 13% bonus might. However, a four-year multi-year annuity with a 4.44% rate might be a marketing disaster in a Chinese-American one.

Imitation

There is a reason why there are a zillion Apple iPods connected to a zillion times two ears and it is largely not due to consumers deciding they had a specific need for a portable music player and then conducting a search to find the optimum solution. No, the main reason for a zillion iPods is imitation. Imitation is why people in sunny climates who never went off-road bought SUVs and why bottled water went from no presence to omnipresent, and because of ecology imitation is becoming of less presence. Consumers like to imitate the behavior of other members of the group to feel a part of the group.

The way imitation can be used to increase annuity is convince consumers that other members of their group use them. This is an area where 3rd party endorsements work well "George Washington said he was proud to own an annuity and that all Americans should buy one" (I made that up). And the size of the market can be used to build a desire for imitating the group "Over a trillion dollars has been placed in annuities" (I did not make that up).

Subliminal Goal Changing

There have been a few academic studies that indicate what a person would typically pay for something may be temporarily changed by first exposing them to unrelated images that suggest a high value or low value. As an example, say the choice is between a $3 Hershey Bar or a $4 Ghirardelli chocolate bar. If the consumer is first shown a Saks Fifth Avenue catalog the consumer would be more likely to pick the $4 chocolate. On the other hand, if the person was handed a Wal-Mart ad they would be more likely to choose the $3 chocolate bar.

The implications are powerful; the problem is I do not have a strong sense of how you translate this into setting the annuity sale. Might having copies of *Worth* or *Fortune* in your waiting area cause a consumer to select more "high value" riders in the annuity offered? Could serving them coffee in fine china cups increase the average sale? I do not have a clue.

> **Setting The Sale**
> • Mimic the consumer by using similar body language
> • Repeat what they say, do not paraphrase
> • Be aware of possible superstitions and act accordingly
> • Consumers like to imitate behavior that makes them feel part of the group so show them the group likes the annuity

Initial Framing

Beat The Bank Not The Market

Whether you call it framing or setting the stage, the lead up to the product presentation is crucial. For example, you could open with "this index annuity has a 7% ceiling on the interest you can earn next year" or you could say "your bank has a 1-year CD rate of 4%; this index annuity has a 7% ceiling." The reason for the later phrasing is to move the client to your financial reality.

The representative needs to build realistic risk and return expectations for the annuity by framing the annuity with positive benchmarks. A good benchmark to use is the bank. The positive aspects of the bank are they provide interest paying savings instruments without stock market risk of loss – the same story as fixed annuities. The good news is banks often pay lower yields than fixed annuities. The point of the framing is to capture the safety message of the bank along with the annuity potential for higher interest. I devote an entire chapter to bank and annuity safety, so for now let us focus on the realistic expectation framing.

<u>"Your bank is paying" versus "The stock market is doing"</u>

Some representatives try to show how good fixed annuities are by talking about stock market investments. By talking about the stock market the annuity benchmark becomes the stock market. If the representative is telling a client that one could lose money in an investment if the stock market goes down, but not in annuity, the framing becomes "stock market losses" and "annuity." If the representative begins an index annuity talk with "S&P 500" or "index-linked interest" the framing is "stock market gains" and "index annuity." The problem is you do not want a consumer to think about losses when presenting a fixed annuity and the index annuity is going to lose if the consumer thinks they are going to fully participate and earn stock market returns. Stock market references are a bad way to open a fixed annuity presentation because they do not act like stock market investments. However, a stock market reference is a good frame for a variable annuity presentation because the frame can be "creating a lower risk stock market" with the variable annuity.

The bank return expectation frame is a win for the representative. Fixed rate annuity returns tend to be very competitive and offer the advantage of tax deferral. Index annuity returns offer the potential of "winning the safe money lottery" by potentially earning two times, three times, or even more interest than the bank is paying today, inside a vehicle that also does not subject the consumer to market risk of principal.

"They" Are Trash-talking Annuities

A negative message is effective, especially if the message is not challenged or if a decision will be made soon after hearing the negative message (which is why more "my opponent is evil" ads appear the week before an election). But if the message is challenged there is a good chance the bad article vibes can be turned or at least neutralized. How? Primarily by attacking the fairness of the article.

144

The mistake often made is trying to refute the negative message with rational counterpoints. The problem is the negative message was not processed rationally by the consumer but was instead felt emotionally. The consumer cannot listen with his head to logic when emotions are in the driver's seat. What one needs to do is directly address the emotional issue because only by neutralizing the emotion is the consumer able to listen to a rational response. You break through the emotional shield by creating a Scooby-Doo moment.

A Scooby-Doo moment results when you say something that makes the consumer stop thinking with their emotions and makes them lift up their head and essentially go "oorrrouh." At this point the emotional wall comes down and the representative can reach the consumer.

Fairness

If an article says fixed annuities have high fees, a lot of consumer complaints, and quotes three mutual funds saying how evil fixed annuities are, the most effective response is say "that is so unfair."

We normally do not like to think of ourselves as unfair and when we hear that something we believe might be unfair we tend to step back and listen to the reasons why. At this point we start thinking rationally and quit thinking emotionally. And at this point the representative can frame the situation.

The first part of the response would be "Yes I read the article; that was so unfair. Why was the reporter so unfair? Why wasn't anyone from the annuity carriers interviewed? I noticed there were 14 mutual fund ads in the reporter's publication and no annuity ads – I wonder who pays the reporter's salary. I wonder if the reporter's maiden name was Fidelity?" followed by major point rebuttals such as "Fixed annuities do not have annual fees. There has only been one FINRA complaint involving fixed annuities in the last two years. Fixed annuities are good because they have guarantees." If the consumer is persuaded the negative attack is unfair, they will ignore it.

The same approach can be used when a competitor badmouths your product. One would bring up points about the competitor that show the consumer the competitor's was unfair and biased. After the emotional negative film has been washed away by the cleansing power of righting unfairness the consumer can rational respond to the points made.

How to Overcome a Really Bad Annuity Attack

A television network reality attack show once tried to send the message that annuities are sold by liars telling lies. Since the advantage of producing your own show means you have total control over what the audience sees they succeeded. There are times when an attack is so vicious and so personal – and so well executed – that one cannot use unfairness. These attacks take a negative point and blow it up so big that it becomes THE major point. The reason it is so effective is their attack contains an element of truth so that you are forced to agree they are right and your response becomes "yeah, but..." which makes it look like you are copping a plea instead of maintaining your innocence. The most effective strategy becomes "they are not talking about me."

Use the Casablanca approach.

Just as Casablanca's Captain Renault told Rick he was shocked that gambling was going on, the representative needs to express shock, shock to hear that the negative points brought up in the attack actually happen in your business. You are delighted that the reporter, celebrity, or politician has brought this out into the open and hope any reprobates stalked and entrapped in the attack are severely punished.

Do not talk about bias or errors in the attack. You may wonder out loud about how many thousands of representatives they had to sift through before they found the ones they selectively showed doing the mischief, but you cannot attack the attack unless

EVERYTHING said in the attack was wrong. The reason why is if you say one aspect of the show was wrong the consumer may think you mean everything else was right. Your position should be that it was a wonderful attack, honest and fair, because...

You are not them

"You know Mr. & Mrs. Consumer the only problem when you hear a story about a bad doctor, bad teacher, bad saint is it tarnishes the reputation of the good people...like me." Unless you are one of the folks caught on camera or mentioned in the indictment the attack did not concern you. You do not operate that way so let us move on and get back to business.

It Usually Does No Good To Try To Correct The Attacker
We see a biased report or article and our first instinct is to contact the source and correct them. However, almost always the reporter or politician knows their report is biased, that is what makes it effective. And if the bias is due to factual errors they usually do not want to publicly correct the errors because they would have to admit they were wrong.

A couple years ago I caught a financial writer repeatedly slamming annuities by printing lies that he had been told by competing securities folks (he let me know his sources). I was able to prove that all of his annuity contentions were wrong. He admitted to me he had been wrong. But he also said he would not print the facts now because his readers would know he had been wrong about annuities and he had a reputation for being truthful.

Trying to get the attacker to publicly admit error or bias very seldom works. You can go the editor and ask, in the interest of fairness, for your rebuttal to be publicized. This will occasionally work, but you may have noticed that rebuttals or corrections are never printed on the front page. The other problem is you risk reawakening an issue that has probably been largely forgotten by everyone except you.

Paint Pictures

More consumers will buy if you create a vivid picture of the benefits of your product than if you simply recite features. I realize this is taught in sales training 101, but it is worth remembering. You could say the annuity will hopefully generate more interest over the years than the savings account, or you could say the annuity will hopefully allow the consumer to spend some time out on a cool summer morning sitting in their 22 foot bass boat (with the inboard jet) reeling in a 6 pound smallmouth bass.

You could talk about how a $20,000 premium could establish the grandchild's college fund, and show slides and charts and graphs on what the $20,000 might grow to and what college costs will be in 2024. Or, you could talk about seeing a bright young adult in cap and gown walking across that stage to receive their degree telling everyone that "I owe all this to my grandparents" (maybe we should put in $30,000 today and try for *magna cum laude*?). Help the consumer anticipate the satisfaction they will enjoy by choosing the annuity.

To Increase Annuity Sales Help Them Visualize The Goal

A recent study suggests that people become more risk averse as they visualize what they will do with their money; this can help shift money to annuities. We usually think about retirement planning in terms of returns. Because financial terms represent abstract concepts – you cannot hold a return in your hands – we try to treat this as a sporting event and "win retirement" by going for the highest return "score."

But the ultimate retirement goal is usually not having the highest quarterly IRA return on the block; instead it is using those IRA dollars to pay for the mortgage, to cover travel, or perhaps to cover the grandchildren's college. When we think about the IRA in terms of what we want it to accomplish we become more concerned about losing that IRA money, because it no longer is an abstract concern but instead a more visceral concern of perhaps being unable to pay the mortgage and losing the house.

If the consumer is missing the big retirement picture by getting overly hung up on scoring in the current financial quarter and possibly losing the financial game, the representative should get the consumer to talk about what they intend to do with the retirement money.

If the goal is to pay the mortgage is the potential to earn a few extra percent enough reason to possibly lose the money for the mortgage payment? Does it make sense to risk the money needed to pay for housing, food and medical care? After the representative helps the consumer cover the basics, perhaps the excess cash can be used to gamble for a few extra percent.

We tend to be riskier with our money when we think about it only as a way of keeping score and not related to actual needs. We become more risk averse when we think about the needs that the money will ultimately be covering.

Consumer Thinks The Return Is Low? Make It Relative

Your account earned 4% last year; how does that make you feel? Without a reference point a 4% return may seem a bit low. But what if everyone else lost 10% last year, now how do you feel?

I talk about reference points in other chapters as well because it is such an important concept. When financial analysts compare returns of the S&P 500 Index with, say, a mutual fund, they usually talk about how the fund performed relative to the S&P 500. In other words, if the S&P 500 gained 10% for a period and the fund gained 11% the analysts would talk about the fund doing 10% better than the index return. The analysts take a recognized benchmark and see how the selected mutual fund did against it. The analysts realize that simply looking at the mutual fund returns without comparing them to a benchmark does not provide a vivid picture of the mutual fund's true performance. The same relative return concept applies to annuities. Using the correct benchmark is an example of framing.

The consumer owns an annuity that produced an 8% return. Their stockbroker told them the XYZ mutual fund earned 14% last year. Why is the annuity return so poor?

There are times when the appropriateness of the frame should be considered. The representative might say "of course that mutual fund that earned 14% last year lost 25% the previous" or possibly say "because the annuity cannot lose credited interest it would be more appropriate to compare that 8% return with the 5% yield you would have earned in the CD."

<u>Valid Frame</u>
The consumer owns a CD that earned 5% last year and the annuity paid 4%.

Challenge the validity of the frame, perhaps by saying "So after taxes both the annuity and CD are compounding a 4%." Another alternative is to frame the returns as a multiple year experience; "there will be times when the CD has higher yields, but the hope is overall the annuity will provide a very competitive return."

1/n – To Increase The Dollars Allocated to Annuities

People often use the simple diversification rule of thumb of allocating assets equally between categories. If one stock account and one bond account are offered this *1/n strategy* (1 divided by the number of choices) places half of the assets in each account.

Calling this a strategy is pushing it because all you are saying is if you have 3 choices you'll put 1/3 in each slot and if you have 10 choices you'll put 1/10 in each. The problems are that allocating everything equally may result in putting too much in some places and too little in others resulting in less than excellent diversity. The second is the individual categories may be too similar to provide sufficient diversity, but the consumer will still be tempted to make equal splits.

A study was done a few years ago that compared allocation choices in two pension plans. One plan offered a selection of 5 stock funds and 1 bond fund, the other offered 1 stock fund and 4 bond funds. At the time the average consumer had 57% of their pension money allocated to stocks. However, consumers in the plan with 5 stock choices had 75% of their money in stocks; consumers in the plan with 4 bond choices had only 34% in stocks and 66% in bonds. In both cases consumers had loaded up a specific asset simply because it had more slots to choose from.

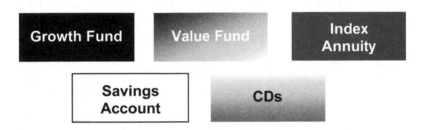

What does this means for annuity representatives? If a consumer has a savings account, a CD, a growth mutual fund, a value mutual fund and an annuity is proposed the consumer may subconsciously think in terms of placing 1/5 of their assets in the annuity because they see 5 choices. But what if the consumer is shown a chart divided into fourths that shows "bank", "mutual funds", "index annuity" and "multi-year annuity"? The 1/n strategy would result suggest half of the assets being placed in annuities.

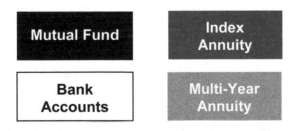

Will relabeling assets cause half of the money to be placed in annuities? I doubt it, but research indicates the annuity slice of the allocation pie should increase.

Consumer Does Not Like Possible Zero Returns

The reality of an index annuity is the index-linked interest may be zero if the index does not cooperate.

I realize "zero is your hero" is a cute saying, but there are a couple problems with that line. The first is trying to get the consumer to believe a falling index is a good thing, and while that may be rationally true it is difficult for us to believe that loss is good on an emotional level. The second problem is we do not truly understand the concept of nothing. We can visualize gains, we can visualize losses, but we have a difficult time comprehending on an emotional level what the absence of gain or loss really means.

The Consumer Anchor

A consumer does not want to buy an index annuity earning anywhere from 0% to a 7% interest cap, because they know they might earn nothing from the annuity next year and the bank is paying 4%.

The Frame

Make doing nothing the biggest loss. It goes like this, "Mr. & Mrs. Consumer, if you buy the index annuity you could lose up to the 4% interest the bank is paying, but if you stay at the bank you will lose the potential to earn up to 7% interest in the index annuity. This really is very simple: Take the annuity and maybe lose 4% or stay put and maybe lose 7%. Which is the greater loss?"

Consumer Does Not Want To Break $50,000 CD

People show a tendency to hold on to money in the form of a whole and a willingness to spend money in the form of parts. Most people are more likely to buy a small item if they have a small bill rather than a large one – if we want to buy a candy bar we would be more likely to purchase it if we had some $1 bills in our wallet than if we had a $100 bill. We tend to value large bills more than small bills as well – a $100 bill makes us feel richer than five $20s – and this value makes us want to preserve it. Understanding this can help make the annuity sales and more the annuitybuyer less likely to exchange to another annuity.

The Consumer Anchor

Consumers subconsciously establish financial anchors in their heads. The difference between $49,990 and $50,000 may be only ten dollars, but in our minds the difference is much greater. If we spend $100 of the first amount we are left with $49,890, but if we spend $100 of the second amount we no longer have $50,000.

A consumer with a matured CD worth $50,000 may be less inclined to buy an annuity than if they had a $48,000 CD because the $50,000 has become the anchor point.

The Frame

The representative does not destroy the anchor but merely replaces it. A simple way is to replace the $50,000 CD anchor is with a $50,000 annuity anchor – the anchor remains only the location has changed.

Another way is to combine anchors so the old anchor amount remains – instead of talking about moving $30,000 to the annuity and leaving $20,000 in the CD emphasize how the new annuity/CD anchor still has a value of $50,000.

Another way is to make the annuity anchor larger by looking into the future – $50,000 in a multi-year annuity earning 4.66% for 4 years replaces the $50,000 CD anchor with a future $60,000 annuity anchor, and $60,000 is bigger than $50,000.

If the representative manages to break the anchor subsequent sales will encounter less resistance. Say the consumer is moving $50,000 from the CD into a money market, waiting for rates to go back up, but agrees to buy a $5,000 annuity and move $45,000 to the money market because this has been framed as the consumer still having $50,000, but in two places. Future annuity sales will be easier because the new bank anchor is $45,000, which is not a strong anchoring point.

Discouraging Future Annuity Replacement

An annuity can be made stickier (less likely to be replaced) by tying it to outside anchors. If an annuity is thought of as part of a whole it becomes a part of much larger anchor. For example, if this annuity is part of a retirement plan that includes other annuities or investments, and the interactions of the whole plan guarantees a successful retirement, it will be difficult to hack out one piece of the total plan – replace the annuity – because the entire plan might collapse.

Alternately the annuities could be structured as a series. If a laddered multi-year strategy is used with annuity term lengths of 4, 5, 6, 7, 8, and 9 years the consumer will be reluctant to disturb any one piece of the series. And because there are multiple surrender periods involved it will be difficult to do multiple replacements without meeting strong resistance.

Another way to discourage replacement is to pay a higher overall yield based on the total annuity assets a consumer has with a carrier. More carriers are paying higher yields for larger premiums within one contract, all this is does pay the yield bonus based on total assets at a carrier. It would be difficult to transfer a $25,000 annuity if the remaining $75,000 in the remaining annuities get their yield cut.

Small Frames

Home Bias

A properly diversified portfolio for an investor should contain investments from many countries, and yet most folks keep most of their money invested in companies from their own country. A lot of this is because we are familiar with our own companies so we stick with names we know.

If your annuity carrier is not a household name it can help by making the consumer think it is. If your annuity carrier is publicly traded pulling up its name on the stock pages helps to show that other people are aware of the company and the consumer should be to. If privately held a company brochure showing employee faces can help the consumer connect with the carrier, and simply repeating the carrier's name often during the sales process makes it more familiar and acceptable.

Short-Term Framing Helps Annuity Sales

Say two consumers look at and adjust their investment portfolio allocations once a year, but Consumer A plans to spend his money in twelve months, while Consumer B will not use the money until 30 years from now. Even if both consumers were fully aware of the long-term stock and bond market returns and risk both consumers would tend to allocate their portfolios the same way – with a strong emphasis in bonds – because their evaluation periods are on 12 month cycles, even though this near-sighted view is costing Consumer B a considerable loss in potential returns.

This short-term approach to long-term horizons has been found to be true for both part-time investors and professional pension managers (because pension managers must show short-term results they also tend to be too risk averse to maximize long-term returns).

The problem is an irrational fixation on the negative possibility of ending the next year with a loss means consumers tend to keep too much money in lower returning instruments that are less volatile. The good news for representatives is consumers are inclined to place more in fixed annuities because of the absence of market loss.

Annuity Buying Framed As Completing A Journey

A deferred annuity is often presented as a retirement vehicle, one that will make available funds to provide income at a future time. The annuity is shown as a solution to a future need. However, it may be better to present retirement planning as a journey that has already begun and the annuity as an essential step

155

needed to complete the journey. A behavioral quirk in most of us means we are more likely to complete a task we have already begun rather than start a new task. If the annuity is presented as a part of process already started – a secure retirement – rather than as a new task – now we buy an annuity – it will more likely be done.

Rather than selling an annuity it is more effective to present the annuity purchase as simply another step. So, maybe Step 1 is checking on Social Security benefits, Step 2 is maximize 401(k) contributions, Step 3 is obtain fixed annuity, Step 4 is buy house by the lake...A secure retirement is simply a matter of following the steps.

A Guaranteed Lifetime Withdrawal Benefit Fable
In the Aesop Fable *The Grasshopper and the Ant* the ant works during the summer putting away resources whilst the grasshopper parties. The next winter the ant uses the stored resources to survive whilst the grasshopper dies. The moral is prepare today for tomorrow.

Some consumers are ants and some are grasshoppers, and most of what I have read says you cannot change a grasshopper into an ant. However, it appears you can briefly affect both the ant and grasshopper's next decisions by showing them what next winter might bring.

The 2008 Bear Market cast doubt on the reliability of the Wall Street retirement income model where you allocate, withdraw a safe rate, and pray. A GLWB allows a grasshopper to receive a higher initial payout than would be suggested by the 3% or 4% "safe" withdrawal rate suggested by many planners so they can have a better party. A GLWB allows an ant to have the flexibility and freedom to take or defer income. The solution for both bugs is an annuity with a guaranteed lifetime withdrawal benefit provides for tomorrow and keeps alive the dream of partying too.

The Final Frame

I have said people buy make decision to feel good or avoid feeling bad. So, is it better to make the annuity purchase appeal to our sunshine "feel good" side or should we frame the annuity as a prevention – wear your mittens – kind of sale?

People buy annuities to avoid feeling bad

Telling the consumer how the annuity can prevent loss, prevent probate, prevent shame, is usually more effective than telling them how good it can be with an annuity. People buy annuities to avoid feeling bad.

Consumers are spoiled. They know they have had a generally good run, so the representative's message could be "a fixed annuity is the grown-up way to handle retirement income needs because you do not want your children to be stuck taking care of you" or more simply, "It is time to grow up, take care of your retirement, and buy the annuity."

Sales Points

> Make the frame valid and relate it to the annuity

> It is much easier to beat the bank than beat the stock market

> The attack on an annuity is unfair

> Use 1/n to increase the annuity sale

> Buying an annuity is simply the next step in retirement planning

> Buy an annuity and avoid feeling bad

Background Sources

Framing
Shiv, Britton, Payne. 2004. Does elaboration increase or decrease the effectiveness of negatively versus positively framed messages. *Journal Of Consumer Research*. 31.6:199-208

Shiv, Huber. 2000. The impact of anticipating satisfaction on consumer choice. *Journal of Consumer Research*. 27.9:202–215

Shiv, Edell, Payne. 1997. Factors affecting the impact of negatively and positively framed ad messages. *Journal Of Consumer Research*. 24.12:285-294

Mimicking & Mirroring
Tanner, Robin etal. 2008. Of chameleons and consumption: The impact of mimicry on choice and preferences. *Journal Of Consumer Research*. 34:754

Superstition
Kramer, Thomas, Lauren Block. 2008. Conscious and nonconscious components of superstitious beliefs in judgment and decision making. *Journal Of Consumer Research*. 34:783

The Final Frame
Aaker, Jennifer, Angela Lee. 2001. "I" seek pleasures and "We" avoid pains: The role of self-regulatory goals in information processing and persuasion. *Journal Of Consumer Research*. 28.6:33-49

Chapter 7 – Objection Preemption

*Do not ask the consumer what their expectations are
– tell them what their expectations should be*

*Do not ask the consumer what their goals for the annuity are –
tell them what their goals should be*

*Preemption is framing the situation so the objection
never comes up in the first place*

The typical sales book talks about overcoming objections and often defines this as a battle between the salesperson's powers of persuasion and the buyer's reluctance to commit. However the "objection" may either be a request for more information – in which case nothing needs to be "overcome" – or a signal that the buyer has already decided not to buy.

For example, if the buyer asks "how long is my money tied up in that annuity" they could simply be trying to decide where the annuity fits in with their other assets. In this case the buyer has subconsciously decided in favor of the annuity purchase and is trying to determine how large a purchase to make. On the other hand, the buyer may have decided not to buy the annuity and the question represents a psychologically acceptable way for the buyer to tell the salesperson no without turning it into a confrontation. I am afraid that much of the advice on how to overcome objections is often ineffective because its goal is to coerce the buyer into reversing their decision, and even when it is successful the final result may be a remorseful annuityowner.

There are many times the consumer does not buy because the product does not help them achieve their goals. Rather than trying to "overcome" and sell the buyer something they do not want, the representative should move on to the next prospect. However, often the reason the consumer does not decide to buy is they simply do not feel they have the necessary facts to make a favorable decision. The consumer needs information that is relevant to them. This definitely does not mean the consumer needs to know everything the representative knows, but only those facts that are important for the consumer. By providing the needed information in a way that shows the consumer how the annuity will help achieve their goals the representative preempts future objections.

Preempting the objection – meaning to address the objection before it arises – may be the best solution.

Preempting the objection is showing the consumer why the annuity fits their goals in spite of the negative aspects of buying the annuity. It is creating a favorable decision-making framework that raises and answers the objections during, or even before, the presentation. It is the exact opposite of the representative waiting until "the close" to find out what information is missing, which is often too late because the consumer has already decided not to buy based on the information they have.

The way in which the relevant information is presented, or framed, usually determines the decision outcome. The framing of the information helps the consumer determine whether the annuity will help them and should be purchased. The rest of this chapter has ideas to help representatives ensure that objections never come up by providing the answer before the question is raised.

Safety (Liquidity)
When I ask representatives why consumers buy annuities the overwhelming response is because fixed annuities are safe. But what is safety? A representative often translates the concept of annuity safety into a lack of stock market risk, but this is not the typical consumer's definition of safety. From my talks with consumers I believe their definition of safety is "can I get my money back?"

The consumer is asking – *can I get my money back (is there market risk)?*

The consumer likes the fact that fixed annuity principal and credited interest cannot be lost if the stock market goes down, but this benefit is important only because it ties into the broader concept of "can I get my money back." For many consumers this no-market-loss benefit is enough, because their definition of safety is not losing money in the stock market.

Objection Preemption: "In a fixed annuity both your principal and credited interest is protected from stock market risk of loss."

The consumer asking – *can I get my money back (are the annuity funds FDIC insured)?*

Occasionally a consumer will get hung up on what happens if the insurance company goes out of business. I found a couple ways that often preempt the concern.

Objection Preemption: If at the start of the presentation the representative writes on a piece of paper the words "CD, fixed annuity, savings bond" and then tells the consumer they will be talking about fixed annuities today, questions about fixed annuity safety often go away. The reason is because the annuity is listed between two instruments that the consumer already feels are safe the consumer mentally transfers the safety to the fixed annuity.

Objection Preemption: "Do you know anyone that has ever lost money in a savings account or fixed annuity? No, because these are safe."

What we are doing is framing the safety concern to financial reality. Because bank instruments and fixed annuities are mentioned together as very safe places – and the consumer reinforced that belief by not remembering anyone that had ever lost

161

money in either – the consumer is less likely to challenge the safety of the fixed annuity. The chapter on safety goes into greater detail about the safety record of both bank products and fixed annuities.

The consumer is asking – *can I get my money back (what are the penalties)?*

In our minds the behavioral impact of a 2% penalty and a 20% penalty are very similar. The deterrent effect of losing 2% interest on a 4% CD or 20% of the fixed annuity value appears to be almost the same in determining whether the consumer keeps the money in place (the higher penalty does sometimes deter the representative from replacement however). I believe consumers are relatively indifferent when it comes to the <u>size</u> of the withdrawal penalties. However, the <u>length</u> of the penalty is something else.

The consumer usually needs to believe the longer penalty period is justified by either greater return potential or that the longer penalty period is normal. In a multiple year guaranteed rate annuity the greater return potential can often be expressed as earning a higher rate as the penalty years increase – an 8-year guaranteed rate pays a higher yield than a 6-year one. Or, it can be expressed as protecting a rate as the penalty years increase – an 8-year guaranteed rate pays a lower yield than a 6-year one because the insurer is sticking their neck out for two more years to protect the yield.

Objection Preemption: "The reason for the surrender period is to get you the higher yield."

This same logic can be extended to index annuities – the 8-year penalty product offers greater index participation than the 6-year product. However, if the representative is presenting annuities with penalty periods of 12 or 15 years a more effective story may be that the reason this annuity has a 15-year penalty period is because this annuity is supposed to have a 15-year penalty.

162

Objection Preemption: "This annuity is for your legacy money."

If the annuity has a surrender penalty charge that is high or long or both the representative should be preparing the consumer during the presentation by talking about fixed annuities as the foundation of the retirement years, or the place for the serious money that the consumer will only touch after everything else is gone, or the fixed annuity is the consumer's "legacy money" that is designed to be left for the next generation. Because the representative said a fixed annuity was "legacy money for the next generation" the consumer should be more receptive to a longer penalty period because mentally they have already determined they are not going to touch the money.

The consumer is asking – *can I get my money back (what is the liquidity)?*

When a consumer asks about liquidity they may not be asking what the penalty period is, but rather does the annuity allow the consumer access to the funds they think they might need.

Objection Preemption: "What additional liquidity might you need from the annuity that would not be met by your other assets?"

The annuity will not be the consumer's only asset. The consumer needs to be reminded that liquidity needs should probably be met by places with lower potential yields first. The representative can address the other liquidity the annuity provides.

- Liquidity means the annuity balance goes to the heirs without penalties
- Liquidity means the consumer can access the money if confined to a nursing home
- Liquidity means the consumer can access 10% a year without liquidity charges

All of these "can I get my money back" concerns should be addressed before the product is introduced because then you will know which product will meet the consumer's real needs.

A big reason for not buying a fixed annuity is because the safety concerns have not been answered. Another reason is the consumer has unrealistic return expectations.

Returns (Realistic Expectations)

I have had representatives tell me that they cannot sell a fixed annuity unless they promise a 10% return; the problem with this is 10% cannot be achieved over the long term. The consumer may need this high return either because they have insufficient assets to support their income needs, or more likely, the consumer's view of the financial world is in fantasyland. In either case the representative needs to quickly acquaint the consumer with financial reality.

Tell the consumer what their expectations should be

Before the consumer can tell the representative what they "need" the representative must frame the correct financial reality. Typically the most effective way to do this is by mentioning bank rates or savings bond rates. The representative needs to establish a starting or anchoring point that reflects financial reality and would begin the conversation by saying something like "Well, let's try to beat the 3% interest your bank is offering."

Objection Preemption: "Let's try to beat the bank."

This causes the consumer's anchor to immediately move much closer to reality. The consumer may "need" 10% but they were just told they are not going to get it, and because the representative established financial reality first it becomes the new anchor (if the consumer speaks first then anything the representative says next becomes a counteroffer and the consumer's anchor barely moves, because now the consumer is having a tug of war with the representative and the consumer is trying to make their reality the winner). What if the consumer must have 10%? Then a fixed annuity is not the answer.

Instead of telling the consumer that "this index annuity has a 7% ceiling on the interest you can earn next year" the representative could say "your bank has a 1-year CD rate of 3%; this index annuity has a 7% cap on the interest you may earn". The representative does not have a clue as to where the consumer's head is anchored, but it is a good bet that it is not anchored where the representative wants it to be. One of the reasons sales are lost is because the representative assumes the consumer is in the same financial reality as the representative, but this is seldom the case. The consumer's financial reality needs to create realistic return expectations.

Confronting Fantasy With Reference Points

The fantasy anchor can be something in the past or something the consumer expects to happen in the future. Presenting a 6% annuity yield in a 4% CD environment should seem like the recipe for an easy sale, but what if the consumer expects CD rates to be 7% sometime next year. If the consumer raises an objection when the annuity is clearly the winner, then the best approach may be to simply ask the consumer "what gives" and hear why the consumer is ignoring reality. Often when we are forced to explain why we are being irrational we become more rational.

I started a crusade several years ago to get people to quit calling them equity index annuities or EIAs and to start calling them fixed index annuities or FIAs. It is not that FIA is a good term (I tried calling them IAs but people thought I was talking about immediate annuities), but that EIA was a bad one because the "equity" word created unrealistic return expectations.

Objection Preemption: Don't use the words option, stock market or index link.

Index annuities are not equities and they do not operate like equities. They do not offer the long-term upside potential of equities but neither do they create the risk of loss of equities. Every time a representative uses stock market language in describing an index annuity the consumer may begin thinking the annuity will produce unreachable gains – and thus be disappointed, or start believing there is stock market risk – and not buy at all. The words used need to reflect the realities of the index annuity.

An index annuity <u>benefits</u> from (not is linked to or participates in) increases in the index.

In truth no index annuity is linked to or participates in the movement of an index. The annuity participates in the crediting method formula used by the index annuity. As soon as the representative implies that the annuity is somehow a substitute or derivative (and that word scares people) for the stock market the representative has lost the message. An index annuity benefits from a rising index.

An I Savings Bond pays a minimum rate of interest (usually), plus the potential for additional interest based on changes in the Consumer Price Index. An I Bond owner benefits from a rising Cost of Living index. An index annuity pays a minimum rate of interest, plus the potential for additional interest based on changes in the index. An index annuity owner benefits from a rising index. And because it is usually a stock index the potential benefit may be much higher that the consumer might receive in the bank.

Objection Preemption: Personalize the benefit of tax-deferred compounding.

I am always a bit goosey about praising the possible tax benefits of any financial instrument because there may not be a benefit. For example, if your total income is under a certain level you may not owe income taxes and it would not matter from a tax standpoint whether the interest income was taxable, tax-deferred or tax-free.

But if the representative can show the consumer how their return is improved by tax-deferral it increases the likelihood of a sale. This means digging into the consumer's tax situation.

If the representative can show the consumer how moving $100,000 out of CDs into a deferred annuity means they will not receive a Form 1099 on the $4,000 of compounding interest saving them $1,000 in income taxes next year the case for the annuity is strengthened. Although someday someone will need to pay taxes on the deferred interest a dollar in the hand today is usually valued more than a dollar received tomorrow. Of course, the representative would tell the consumer to get tax advice from their personal advisor.

Objection Preemption: Show the money.

Promises are one thing, delivery is another. While it is wonderful to talk about potential returns it is more effective to show results. Copies of statements showing how the annuity being discussed has performed are powerful tools and add both credibility and a reason to buy. If the annuity offered is new an annuity interest crediting history from the carrier will show how the insurer has treated other customers. The consumer should also be reminded that past performance is no guarantee or indication of future results.

Zero Interest

A reality of index annuities is if the index does not cooperate the annuity could earn zero index-linked interest for the period. Although "zero is your hero" is a cute phrase the reality is the consumer needs to be convinced that a probable zero is not a bad thing

Objection Preemption: Three ways to show why zero is a good choice.

1. State there are many spins of the financial wheel. Unless the consumer is going to take all of their money out and spend it next year it does not make sense to keep their money in a place with the lower possible return simply because a zero might occur every once in a while. The index annuity may come up with zero on any single spin but over time offers the potential for a higher yield.

2. Make doing nothing the biggest loss. The consumer is focused on the potential loss of interest they would have earned with, say, the bank, if it turns out the index annuity credits zero; their concept of loss needs to change. It goes like this "Mr. & Mrs. Consumer if you go into the index annuity you may lose the 4% the bank would have yielded, but if you stay with the bank you will lose the potential to earn the 8% interest (referring to the cap) the index annuity offers. So the decision is move and maybe lose 4% or stay put and maybe lose 8%."

3. Minimize the fear of zero annuity interest by putting the annuity purchase in context. Due to Mental Accounting people segment money into separate pots and do not consider the total outcome. A consumer considering moving $50,000 from a 4% CD to an index annuity may be only seeing the possible loss of $2,000 of CD interest. However, if they are shown a chart reflecting the $50,000 annuity as only a small part of their total $300,000 in interest-earning assets, and shown that if they buy the annuity the total interest income would be between $10,000 and $14,000 instead of the total $12,000 currently received, they are more likely to buy the annuity because it is no longer a choice between earning 100% or earning nothing.

The Policy

Annuity policies are written by lawyers, so naturally they can be difficult to read, impossible to understand and may scare consumers into asking for a refund.

Objection Preemption: Go through a specimen policy during the presentation.

The representative should cover the potential points of concern by going through a specimen policy of the annuity during the presentation (explain that the minimum guarantee table is the worse case example – and not the projection – of what they can earn and the age 95 maturity date is not the surrender period).

Trouble In The Exchange

The representative gets the paperwork signed to move the money from the bank, broker/dealer or variable annuity to the new fixed annuity. A few days later the consumer calls to say their banker/stockbroker/other agent called and the consumer has decided not to go through with the transfer.

What can be done to stop the first counselor from killing the deal? You can warn the consumer that the original counselor will try to stop the transfer, but many representatives have told me that this warning does not help.

Objection Preemption: Trust & avoiding confrontation.

This problem has two aspects. First, it is often a trust issue. The representative often has a new relationship with the consumer, contrasted with a longer term relationship with the first counselor. The words of the first advisor will carry greater weight, unless the consumer is convinced that the representative is more trustworthy and building trust usually takes time.

The second aspect is a desire by the consumer to avoid confrontation. Financial counselors can be seen as authority figures and many people are uncomfortable confronting authority figures. Perhaps the representative should ask the consumer, "will it make you uncomfortable when the first counselor calls you to try to change your mind?" If the answer is yes the representative could suggest some non-confrontational responses such as "the transfer is due to a personal matter that I do not want to discuss." Unfortunately, I do not have hard research on how best to handle this problem.

Putting It All Together

Using objection preemption a representative might begin the presentation like this:

"I have written on this piece of paper the words 'CD, fixed annuity, savings bond' and what we will be talking about today are fixed annuities. In a fixed annuity both your principal and credited interest are protected from market risk of loss. So, let's try to beat the bank!

This annuity has very favorable long-term benefits and should be used as legacy money – the serious money that you will only touch after everything else is gone. Of course you will always have free access to 10% a year of the annuity value and the entire value is available if you enter a nursing home. With that in mind what additional liquidity might you need from the annuity that would not be met by your other assets?

I noticed that your bank is renewing your one year CD at 4%, this annuity will credit 4.5% interest next year (or, this annuity gives you the potential to make up to a cap of 7% interest next year because it benefits from increases in an index). What are your goals for these annuity dollars?"

The representative has spent one minute framing the fixed annuity as a safe place for long-term money with the potential to earn more interest than the bank would pay, and only <u>after</u> this initial framing is completed is the consumer asked what they want. This framing accomplishes a couple of things.

The first is the representative has highlighted the three major annuity objections that are sometimes raised – Safety, Liquidity, and Returns. If the consumer has significant concerns about any part of the objection trinity they will probably say something now and this allows the representative to adjust their presentation. As an example, if the consumer says, "my sister lost a hundred grand in her annuity when the market went down" the representative can address the differences between fixed and variable annuities.

The second point is by talking first and framing what a fixed annuity is the representative is not put in a position where the consumer needs to be confronted or embarrassed. If the representative starts with the question "what are your goals for these annuity dollars?" the consumer could say they are looking for an FDIC insured annuity that pays 8% with no penalties for early withdrawal. It is not a good start if the representative needs to explain how wrong and dumb the consumer is.

Possible Objections

A representative cannot preempt every objection by covering them during the presentation, but if the presentation opens with the proper framing of safety, liquidity and creating realistic return expectations any objections can usually be handled before they become firmly anchored, or the potential objection may be avoided by taking the presentation down another path.

Sales Points

> Preempt the objection by covering the major areas of safety and returns in the opening statement

> Probe to see what "can I get my money bank" really means

> Walk consumers through a sample policy and the steps in an annuity exchange to avoid surprises

Index